INTENT

THE KNOWN PARADIGM

by Hugh Carter Donahue

© Hugh Carter Donahue

CONTENTS TABLE OF CONTENTS

DEDICATION

For Constance & Michael Erlanger and Michael Harold

FOREWORD

by David M. Rowe, Ph.D.

The Internet emerged in a world where computer cycles, memory storage and communication capacity were relatively scarce resources. As a result, minimizing the use of these resources was a primary consideration. Largely because of this, responsibility for information security was assigned to users rather than being built into the core of the system itself. This arrangement was sufficient when the Internet was used by a relatively small group of sophisticated professionals but has become a serious problem as the Internet has evolved into the default platform for use by the general public. Of particular significance, the precursor to the Internet was intended for communication and was not designed to support wide-spread use as a transaction platform with secure exchange of value.

A partial list of positive implications of the rapid evolution of computing and the Internet over the past thirty years must include:

- Ready access to information and learning resources on a scale never before imagined.
- Dramatic acceleration in the ability to review complex issues within far flung organizations and to reach required decisions rapidly.
- Loosening the hold of central physical locations, achieving, at least in part, the promised "the death of distance."
- Changes in the way we shop (Amazon), travel (Airbnb), conduct archival research (Google), perform fulfillment services (FedEx, UPS), and many more.
- Availability of enhanced tools for staying in touch with family and friends.
- Advancement of artificial intelligence capabilities that promise greater insights into extremely complex issues such as protein folding and genetic predisposition to many diseases.

Negative implications include, in part:

- Loss of privacy, driven by an advertising revenue model based on the Devil's Bargain of surrendering personal details to massive search and social media firms in exchange for "free" access to valuable tools for navigating the explosive expansion of on-line information.
- The emergence of cyber security as a constant concern and its failures causing real economic damage.
- A growing addiction to social media that hampers many people's interpersonal communication skills and too often fosters participants' worst instincts, as people feel free to spew venomous comments behind a cyber veil of

anonymity or the comfort of a surrounding mob of likeminded and equally un-self-regulated denigrators.

- A declining ability of many young people to muster the sustained attention needed to master difficult topics.

All the above is widely recognized and discussed in various public forums. What is not as well recognized is that emerging technological innovations are destined to usher in new and comparably dramatic changes in the next few years. These innovations will not resolve all the negative implications highlighted above, but they will have significant impact on two of the most serious, namely: privacy and cyber security.

These innovations will enable a world where individuals own and control their person data and are able to set ground rules for how those data can be used and how individuals will be compensated for such use by others. They will enhance privacy and data security. They will enable a form of compensated disclosure that can create new markets for the data themselves that are not possible in the current technological environment, and they can dramatically improve the efficiency of existing markets.

Introduction

A fresh Paradigm for Internet and 21st Century Commerce & Communications

With widely esteemed acuity, David M. Rowe, Ph.D. identifies a fresh system of general computing, the Known Paradigm, measuring and harnessing intent to clarify and transform the ways we create wealth with data and meta data.

Intent gains increasing value as digital currencies make it ever more feasible and less costly for data and meta data to become elements of money and currencies.

Known Paradigm information technology and digital currency innovations now originate intent as a fresh network element powering 21st century reciprocity.

Transparency can now flourish as a network effect rationalizing Internet and 21st century commerce and communications. This animating, historic achievement enlivens data and meta data.

Efficient, transparent markets can now transact dynamic data and meta data to generate wealth, report taxes and suppress and police fraud.

Technologists, investors and adopters can now create standards to iteratively invent, develop, reliably measure and authenticate the integrity of mass-produced data and meta data and to transact digital currencies transparently.

Individuals, enterprises and institutions can now control, monetize and reciprocally compensate one another for data and meta data that all create with investments, transactions and Internet and broadband communications at no marginal cost.

Competitive interactive computer services (CICS) can now liberate and liberalize Internet and 21st century commerce and communications.

Data and meta data transparencies clarify the monetary and risk values of any specific transaction at any point in time from origination through maturity.

A Living Contract™ authenticates the value that individuals, enterprises and institutions transact as they wish, with whom they wish, when they wish.

An immutable record memorializes each and all transactions.

Responding to the coronavirus pandemic, the Known Paradigm generates income, provides liquidity, clarifies risks sourcing materials, managing logistics and expediting supply chains.

The paradigm reduces bitcoin transaction costs, expedites mining, and it innovates methods to address proof of work and proof of stake.

With the paradigm's generative scale and downwardly compatible scope, egalitarian wealth through data and meta data mass production may initially complement and could eventually superannuate relevance.

The pernicious trade-offs of surrendering privacy for communication efficiency become inefficient. Chasing stochastic consumption acts and narrowly defined monitoring indicators become too costly.

The dominion that Microsoft, Alphabet/Google, Facebook and large network operator incumbents established as commercial Internet and broadband first movers may typify the past, but no longer defines present and future. The same is true for too-big-to-fail banks and their domination over finance.

Nonbank payment service providers like large information technology and financial technology firms, retail chains and regional and national transportation enterprises are cultivating cashless payments[1]. This complements the emergence of intent as a network element and of transparency as a network effect. The same is true of the planned obsolescence of cookies.

Rowe's sagacity is especially timely as more and more calls come forward for egalitarian Internet and broadband data wealth. Andrew Yang, a 2020 Democratic presidential nomination candidate, campaigned that individuals, enterprises and institutions should share in the economic value and determine the privacy of their data and meta data. Senators John N. Kennedy (R-Louisiana) and Josh Hawley (R-Missouri)[2] are initiating federal legislation for statutory provisions for individual, enterprise and institutional data ownership. Paradigm capabilities afford real and near real time clarifications of data and meta data value more efficaciously than currently proposed legislative and regulatory remedies. In June, 2019, Senators Mark Warner (D-Virginia) and Josh Hawley (R-Missouri) proposed legislation introducing transparency into the advertising paradigm. The proposed legislation obligates data disclosures to the Security and Exchange Commission and Federal Trade Commission. Consequent sunlight would then trigger competition, the senators assert. Legislative and regulatory remedies would begin three and one-half years after enactment. Senator Ron Wyden's (D-Oregon)[3] legislation increases privacy protections and impels dominant incumbents to offer fee-based services, which would not harvest data and meta data. In addition to competition regulation, Senator Elizabeth Warren (D-Massachusetts)[4] advocates turning Google, Amazon and Facebook into what she calls "platform utilities" structurally separated from owning content on their services. Governor Gavin Newsom (D-California) advocates a "data dividend" for individual, enterprise and institution data and meta data. State attorney generals and governors are pursuing anti-trust and structural separation initiatives with dominant commercial Internet incumbents. For all the beneficent intent embodied in many of these proposals, most afford palliative remedies requiring accompanying regulatory and compliance costs. Calls for structural separation and breaking up dominant incumbents are now increasingly commonplace.

The great wager in virtually all this beneficently intended legislation and regulation is whether late 19th and early 20th century anti-trust reforms addressing industrial capitalism within nation states can be reworked for 21st century digital economies operating at global scale. The hope is that updated, fine-tuned embodiments of Treasury Secretary George B. Cortelyou's anti-trust enforcement (1907-1909) for

President Theodore Roosevelt (1901-1909) will be effective addressing dominant first mover Alphabet/Google, Apple, Amazon, Microsoft, Facebook and Netflix concentrations in very different economies and technology dynamics.

PUTTING THE SCREWS ON HIM.

Source: https://sites.google.com/a/wayland.k12.ma.us/progressive-era-apush-2016/trustbusting

A May, 2020 Amazon tweet rejoining former Vice President Joe Biden on taxation typifies standard terms of debate. One or another variant of Progressive public policy will solve the problem although one or another expression of Progressive public policy animated it.

> **Amazon Policy** ✔ @amazon_policy · May 22   ⌄
> .@JoeBiden We pay every cent owed. You spent 3 decades in the Senate & know that Congress wrote these tax laws to encourage companies to invest in the US economy. We have. 500k jobs w/ a min wage of $15/hr across 40 states. Assume your complaint is w/ the tax code, not Amazon.
>
> > 🔵 **Joe Biden** ✔ @JoeBiden · May 22
> > I've said it before, and I'll say it again: No company pulling in billions of dollars in profits should pay a lower tax rate than firefighters and teachers.
> >
> > It's time for Amazon to pay its fair share. cnbc.com/2020/05/22/i-t...
>
> ○ 3.9K   ⇄ 23.3K   ♡ 68.7K   ⬆

Distinct economic and technological forces shaping the 2020's are readily visible. For instance, "from the late 1980s through the early 2000s, global merchandise export growth was usually double that of world GDP growth. But during four of the past five years, goods trade growth lagged global GDP growth," U.S. Secretary of Commerce Wilbur Ross[5] observed at the Oxford Union, in February, 2020. "Globalization had gotten out of control. It takes 200 suppliers in 43 countries on six continents to make an iPhone. Global trade growth likely turned negative in 2019 while GDP increased by nearly 3 percent, their first move in opposite directions." Amid these dynamics, "the Fourth Industrial Revolution, or 4IR, is the expanded analytical capability generated by the 5G and the Internet of Things, and it is ushering in a new age of productivity, efficiency, customization, and sustainability. Fourth Industrial Revolution technologies and sustainability will...disrupt those economies that lack highly trained workers," he asserted.

In these circumstances, the best of economic conditions, legislation and regulation are perpetual catch-up. Presidents as distinct as Donald Trump and Barack Obama each concur "the old ways of doing things just don't work" in former President Obama's turn of phrase as political strategist Adam Goodman[6] pointed out in a thoughtful May, 2020 commentary.

Nor do President Trump and former president Obama have any monopoly on this orientation. "There are challenges that we may not meet, that we may not be able to handle, but that require we do things differently. There are no examples for ... the United States or for rich countries generally. Nobody has been in this situation before. So we have to figure it out if we want to survive. There are no models...," political scientist Frances Fox Piven[7] remarked of revolutionary change in June, 2020.

No sooner, however, had Ross and others meeting at the World Economic Forum prognosticated fourth industrial revolution innovation and economic growth then the coronavirus pandemic shut down international markets and suffocated all the oxygen[8] till then energizing flourishing global, regional and national economies in winter.

Giving fresh emphasis to T. S. Eliot's "April is the cruellest month" from The Waste Land burial of the dead passages, historic unemployment, economic warfare[9] and contractions, central bank 0% and negative interest rates, emergency economic stimulus, health care and equipment legislation, shuttering thriving businesses, quarantining the healthy and forbidding attendance at religious services became norms as nations and communities grappled with public health and economic activity. Thirty-one eight million cases and 961,352 deaths, including 6.7 M cases and nearly 200,000 deaths in the USA, afflicted the world at the beginning of autumn, 2020. Economic costs range from $1T[10] to $4T[11] to estimates of $82T[12]. "For the fiscal year, Richemont [the second largest luxury watch manufacturer following LVMH] estimates the coronavirus damage at around €800 million ($882 million) in lost sales," Hodinkee noted in May, 2020. "For the first five months of 2020, Macao casinos have generated $4.135 billion (U.S.) compared with $15.749 billion in the first five months of 2019, a 73.7 percent decline" and hit a record low for June, The Las Vegas Review Journal reported in June and July, 2020[13].

Everything became brand new. Much like Pearl Harbor or 9-11 terror attacks or a boxer's sucker punch, "life has changed dramatically for all of us," Prince Harry[14] remarked in YouTube comments to Invictus competitors on the day of the cancelled opening ceremony as the world grappled with the lethal virus and began coming to initial terms resuming commercial life where possible in May, 2020.

Much of it is scary. "The overall policy response to date has provided a measure of relief and stability, and will provide some support to the recovery when it comes," Federal Reserve Board Chairman Powell[15] remarked. "But the coronavirus crisis raises longer-term concerns as well. The record shows that deeper and longer recessions can leave behind lasting damage to the productive capacity of the economy. Avoidable household and business insolvencies can weigh on growth for years to come. Long stretches of unemployment can damage or end workers' careers as their skills lose value and professional networks dry up, and leave families in greater debt. The loss of thousands of small- and medium-sized businesses across the country would destroy the life's work and family legacy of many business and community leaders and limit the strength of the recovery when it comes. These businesses are a principal source of job creation—something we will sorely need as people seek to return to work. A prolonged recession and weak recovery could also discourage business investment and expansion, further limiting the resurgence of jobs as well as the growth of capital stock and the pace of technological advancement. The result could be an extended period of low productivity growth and stagnant incomes," he forecautioned that May. However, unemployment fell in May as the economy added 2.5 million jobs[16].

The coronavirus inflicts a health crisis, which wrecks an economic crisis that provokes a liquidity crisis potentially triggering a solvency crisis, globally. Bankruptcies[17] will likely swell. The nostrum 'we can print money, because we can' is only good so long till 'we can't.' No one knows when or if such a day will come. It may. It may not. The dollar remains the strongest fiat currency. And, one has to wonder how long massive tax obligations on astronomical debt with zero or net-zero or negative central bank monetary policy and interest rates can be accommodated till enough people say enough and opt for something else. It's always something to think about tomorrow[18].

The Known Paradigm offers critical life lines generating income and providing liquidity through reciprocal buying and selling of permissioned, transparent data and meta data. There can be few better ways to address economic stagnation, imposed by self-quarantine and anticipated metered-apart work rules, and 0% Federal Reserve rates than mechanisms enabling individuals, enterprises and institutions to create wealth buying and selling data and meta data they routinely produce. Transparency obligations and reciprocity incentives police and suppress fraud.

Due to all the information dynamically, reciprocally and transparently placed on its platforms, Known Paradigm transaction currencies afford mechanisms to cope with the volatility of inflation and deflation of fiat currencies, a potential outcome of protracted economic recovery under the conditions of ongoing central bank monetary policies and national government fiscal policies coping with the virus.

Thanks to paradigm capabilities clarifying data and meta data, specifically abilities to see their monetary and risk values, KNOWN technologies ground the 21st century gold standard. In the comparable ways that everyone participates in the notion that a dollar equals one hundred pennies, Known paradigm transparencies show any one participating in any transaction its value at any time. Its information, which is completely visible, constitutes value for any party in addition to the value of any transaction.

As such, Known paradigm technologies afford trust, the most precious element in commerce, at exactly the moment trust in fiat currencies is most attenuated.

"Without trust, there is no money," Steven Longenecker, publisher of American Consequences, observed in May, 2020. "The value of the dollar depends entirely on all of us continuing to believe in it. Without trust, paper currency is nothing more than worthless colored rags.... When trust dies, there is also no accessible credit. The plastic cards in your wallet won't work like you expect. You won't be able to get a mortgage or a business loan at a reasonable rate. Without trust, all the things that we believe in here in America start to fall apart. Without trust, there is no fair rule of law. There is no safe community. There is no prosperous Main Street. There is no opportunity on Wall Street. And there is no investment in the future,"[19] he remarked.

It is impossible to revert to gold without destabilizing currencies and impoverishing masses of individuals, enterprises and institutions.

Yet, entering the third decade of the 21st century, individuals, enterprises and institutions generate, and will continue to create, voluminous data and meta data, which KNOWN technologies refine to transparent wealth and trustworthiness.

Furthermore, Known Paradigm refining creates wealth by enabling individuals, enterprises and institutions to pay themselves, essentially, with data and meta data they transact with Known digital currencies. This is phenomenal, perhaps the paradigm's signal contribution to the 21st century, particularly if adopters deploy paradigm capabilities to address inequities and remediate systemic inequalities.

In these catastrophic circumstances, the Known Paradigm also addresses logistics, supply chains and food supply, which may emerge as enduring coronavirus outcomes and challenges as well. From meat packing cities to big city retail meat shortages to local dairies to fast food restaurants to homeland security concerns to 'Made in USA' filters, paradigm capabilities clarify risks to manage logistics and expedite supplies. Each and all will likely become more consequential and routine going forward as citizens and industry will demand proximity and national sourcing of materials, managing logistics and expediting supply chains. For instance, as medical products become more complex and technological uncertainty characterizes their design and development, the Known Paradigm smooths early supplier involvement to maximize engineering efficiencies and to control costs.[20]

Paradigm capabilities enhance logistics and supply chains advancing the Trump Administration coronavirus vaccine initiative, Operation Warp Speed.

Globally, "multiple teams are working on a coronavirus vaccine, with the hope that several could be approved in record speed. Billions of doses will need to be manufactured, meaning collaboration between industry, regulators and the scientific community will be crucial. The vaccine needs to be available in all parts of the world,"[21] the World Economic Forum observed in May, 2020. Hence, the paradigm's great utility. Beyond accelerating innovation, paradigm capabilities address regulatory concerns: "through the Antitrust Division's PCSF and other tools, we will hold accountable individuals and companies that use the pandemic as an opportunity to engage in criminal antitrust violations,"[22] DOJ Antitrust remarked in June, 2020.

No sentient person could deny that the USA, the sleeping giant, is now awake, at full production on scales not seen since the Second World War, committed to self-reliance. In April, 2020, the Ford Motor Car Company had "never built a single ventilator" yet by mid to late May, it is prepared "to produce one ventilator per minute,"[23] President Trump remarked at Ford's Rawsonville Components Plant. An export market awaits the life-saving medical devices. One hundred thousand ventilators will be stock-piled. All of these ventilators will have to be matched to suppliers, distributors, hospitals and patients, worldwide.

The Known Paradigm now supports an efficient, digital commerce ecology integrating IT and logistics for these machines, and all others.

In other words, paradigm capabilities accelerate the reshoring of manufacturing.

One would be naïve to think supply chains can be easily altered. Many years of investment and manufacturing have gone into their creation in nations with lax environmental laws and lower regulatory costs, no craft and industrial unions and labor costs well below those in the United States. So, creating new America-sourced supply chains will require exceptional efficiencies and efficacies of the sorts that the Known Paradigm so extensively affords. This, too, may be a consequential contribution to 21st century well-being not simply for specific participants in one or another supply chain but for consumer welfare, national income and fiat and digital currencies attending their renaissance. "The coronavirus pandemic slashed to smithereens extended global supply chains and the trend towards deglobalization will have significant impact on the dollar, inflation and digital currencies,"[24] Patrick Tan observed in June, 2020.

The Known Paradigm affords speed, efficiency, security and reliability across all these parties and operations principally, but not exclusively, with ledger technologies that are downwardly compatible with incumbent software systems and intellectual property regimes. These robust functionalities move data, regardless of format or technology, from any number of sources to their destinations through secure, encrypted distributed ledger platform.

Most importantly, however, by rewarding intent, the Known Paradigm paths ways beyond relevance and the advertising paradigm, which impose binary choice, yes or no decision making as daily operating procedure. In the process of engaging Internet and broadband communications, individual, enterprise and institution must submit to vast, exquisite behavioral micro-manipulations engineered to deflect intent into a vast consumption machine. In the process, consciousness becomes confounded for the commercial ends of advertising.

The Known Paradigm, by contrast, is fresh and new. It cultivates consciousness. By rewarding individual, enterprise and institution intent, the paradigm expands decision making to all the ranges and types of choices that one may choose to cultivate expressing consciousness and to create wealth in the process.

KNOWN technologies simplify online shopping and robot and drone deliveries.

KNOWN capabilities boost cloud computing and Internet of Things data accuracy and data sharing to support efficient sourcing and supply chains.

KNOWN capabilities speed 5G mobile services. "The adoption of 5G will increase the cost of compatible devices and the cost of data plans," the World Economic Forum pointed out in a May, 2020 Covid Action Platform briefing.[25] Known Paradigm design enabling individuals, enterprises and institutions to buy and sell data and meta data incentivizes adoption of speedier, robust mobile devices and plans at higher price points by rewarding adopters, and paradigm capabilities governing permission restrain autocratic control. The paradigm breathes fresh oxygen into every system and transaction.

In late May, as the country was making headway with phased reopenings to move beyond the coronavirus, a pandemic of civil disorder and social unrest erupted following the death of George Floyd, an African-American pleading 'I can't breathe,' at the knee of a Minneapolis, Minnesota police officer, who was responding to a complaint that Floyd had allegedly paid for cigarettes with a counterfeit twenty dollar bill and with whom Floyd had worked as a security guard at a nearby night club. Widespread urban looting, arson, assault, lawlessness, destruction, attempted destruction of police vehicles and vandalism exploited and overtook demonstrations. The brightest economic news that the number of unemployment applications had for the first time fallen from the preceding week since coronavirus onset got no air occurring, as it did, at the same instance as pervasive, urban arson, looting and vandalism.

President Trump, as is his custom, employed Twitter to alert the nation that he had communicated with the Floyd family and expressed his condolences to them, indicate his insistence on a full investigation of police conduct and to communicate that law enforcement would suppress civil disorder, rioting, looting and arson as e exploitations of his death and memory.

Twitter, then, annotated and masked-over the last sentence of one of President Trump's tweets ("These THUGS are dishonoring the memory of George Floyd, and I won't let that happen. Just spoke to Governor Tim Walz and told him that the Military is with him all the way. Any difficulty and we will assume control but, when the looting starts, the shooting starts. Thank you!") on editorial grounds.[26] Twitter had earlier annotated a tweet on mail-in voting with an exclamation mark to designate it as false.[27] By so doing, Twitter forestalled likes and shares. "The offence of forestalling the market is… an offence against public trade," Blackstone observes (Commentaries Laws of England, Volume IV, p 158) " by dissuading persons from bringing in their goods."

With this curation, Twitter prosecuted a denial of service far beyond its congressionally delegated discretion. Nothing in enabling legislation authorizes an interactive computer service to regulate, define, curtail or suppress likes or sharing. Nor does Twitter enjoy any particular claim to algorithmic recommendation, as it is a conduit for information content providers.

Twitter, like Facebook and You Tube, is legally designated as an interactive computer service under Section 230 of the Communications Decency Act of 1996. In return for "Good Samaritan" blocking of offensive content, Twitter and other interactive computer services receive a limited liability shield for content that individuals, enterprises and institutions post to their service platforms: i.e., "No provider or user of an interactive computer service shall be treated as the publisher or speaker of any information provided by another information content provider."[28] As long as Twitter suppressed "material that the provider or user considers to be obscene, lewd, lascivious, filthy, excessively violent, harassing, or otherwise objectionable, whether or not such material is constitutionally protected" including sex trafficking, the limited liability shield insulated and inoculated it from torts of defamation. Billions of dollars of revenues rolled into Twitter and other California firms offering interactive computer services.

Twitter's editorial decision suppressing one and annotating another Trump tweet, well after it had flagged none of Congressman Adam Schiff's tweets regarding Russia or impeachment and, in fact, had hired a vehement critic of the president as independent content arbiter, rankled.

So much so, President Trump embraced Progressive public policy to issue an executive order preventing online censorship.[29]

By suppressing and annotating the president's tweets, Twitter took a risk, embraced the sword of Emile Zola's J'Accuse and chucked its Good Samaritan liability shield. It crossed the Rubicon and proclaimed itself a publisher.[30] It emphatically marked a fresh identity as an editor cultivating a partisan orientation by abandoning its congressionally delegated discretion as an interactive computer service. After all, "the liberty of the press is not understood to imply absence of liability to judicial punishment for the publication of libelous or criminal matter, nor to be inconsistent with the right of the courts to prohibit a particular publication as involving a wrong to some person," The Oxford English Dictionary defines, and it is precisely this Pandora's Box that Twitter opened.

By scrutinizing the platform limited liability shield, the executive order opens up contract protections for fresh thinking and implementation where Known paradigm capabilities are especially salutary.

Known Paradigm digital currency, living contractsTM and immutable records would enable Facebook, Google for its YouTube platform and Twitter to migrate toward contract protections amid looming torts of defamation.

For Facebook, Google and Twitter, the paradigm immunizes and inoculates boycotts. By removing their dependency of advertising, all could focus on core services and institutional mission undistracted by partisans attempting to cow management.

A boycott attempts to destroy or cancel a brand. It seeks logarithmic effects from one or another incident. For Facebook, boycotts subvert the polite fiction of one big, happy, trustworthy family. Instead, if a Facebook advertisement appears for a consumer durable or one or another product is now somehow or other being shamed (say, canned goods and packaged foods), other Facebook advertisements are concomitantly diminished, sullying Facebook as no longer the gold standard of trustworthiness as well as whatever injury is imposed on the targeted brand. Facebook's dependency on wholesale advertising cedes this inflecting power to any and all partisans seeking to exploit its network effects for partisan advantage. Nowhere is Facebook dominance in wholesale advertising more visible as its Achille's heel, too, than 2020 boycotts. Why go to Facebook when it accommodates individuals, enterprises or institutions plausibly accused of one or another allegedly shameful violation of contemporary norms, someone could conjecture? That seed of doubt is adequately virulent to scare off advertisers.

It does not have to be this way. The Known Paradigm affords a new model. Intent boosts volumes and increases asset values.

At the other end of capital accumulation, the Known Paradigm affords wealth creation by the poorest, those enduring systemic adversities. Indeed, KNOWN capabilities enable adopters to innovate narrowly-tailored, directly-targeted marketplace solutions, focused on equality-generating opportunities as well as transactions utterly agnostic to race, class or national origin, which may well lift the nation out of divisive, discriminatory legacies.

It is important to emphasize the egalitarian nature of any such initiatives. Individuals, enterprises and institutions can employ paradigm transparencies to increase their wealth and advance their economic equality. At heart, the paradigm rewards sagacious risk. Through its sedulous monitoring and unimpeachable tracking, the Known Paradigm animates crushing advantage.

In so far as network operator, social media, search, operating system, entertainment and advertising industries both create and extract wealth from individual, enterprise and institution data and meta data, fiduciaries[31] could emerge as clearing houses returning some of the wealth to them all.

As Rowe foresees, the Known Paradigm and its new system of general computing would rationalize markets for the broadest benefits for the widest numbers of persons, enterprises and institutions.

Chapter One introduces intent as an original network element and transparency as a network effect powering the innovations.

Chapter Two explains that internal vulnerabilities and negative externalities so barnacle relevance and the advertising paradigm that it now in the public interest to move beyond the commercial Internet.

Chapter Three details Known Paradigm efficiencies and efficacies stimulating 21st century wealth among its many other benefits to society and humanity.

Intent: A Fresh Network Element

CHAPTER ONE

Intent: A Fresh Network Element

Known Paradigm information technology and digital currency innovations now identify intent as an original network element scaling Internet and broadband mass production through fresh individual, enterprise and institution capabilities to own, control, buy and sell data and meta data.

With this historically distinct achievement, the Known Paradigm creates:

- 21st century reciprocity enriching abilities for individuals and organizations to control, monetize, and compensate one another for the data and metadata that all create with daily on-line and mobile communications.

- new architectural efficacies and efficiencies

Intent embodies technological innovation.

Intent is all present and future.

Intent expresses gratifying, rewarding, beneficial actions that are contemplated to transpire in the immediate or prospective future. *The Oxford English Dictionary* distinguishes intent's essentially prospective ideation and activity as follows: "the act or fact of intending or purposing; intention, purpose (formed in the mind)…will, inclination; that which is willed, pleasure, desire." Late Latin *intentus* for attention, old French *entent* for application and *entente* for desire fuse to form its meaning.

The Known Paradigm innovations are transformative, wide ranging and comprehensive. They allow individuals and organizations to maintain control over the terms of use for their own data and metadata and to enforce the level of privacy they desire. They enable peer-to-peer data transactions of any type. They provide incentives based on proof-of-value. For each transaction, Known Paradigm innovations enforce contractual relationships that are mutually agreed upon and continuously updated. Because the innovations are agnostic across structure, these capabilities record detailed analytics for each transaction across platforms and applications requiring little or no programming. Immutable records document every transaction.

By rationalizing intent, the paradigm activates fresh network elements organically to scale interoperability and downward compatibility across distributed networks, archives and applications to maximize the value, volume and velocity of data assets, products and services. "Each and every recurrence adds individual, enterprise, institution and systemic value," Constance Erlanger, KNOWN™ CEO and Founder remarks.

"I created the inventive methods initially to incent transparency when brokering investment vehicles. Too many transactions failed either because one or another party could not assess risk satisfactorily due to opaque information. Parties could not trust their own judgement of the risk of an investment. I set to originating technologies that create trust by rewarding all parties for sharing information. Risks become clearer and more accurately measurable. With digital information so widely deployed and digital currency innovations coming into broader use, intent can now scale communications and finance," Michael Erlanger, KNOWN™ Founder observes.

Original capabilities display actual values of distinct cryptocurrencies transacting through specific block chains. This historic achievement grounds stable, secure chains, coins and tokens to support trust and risk through rationalizing cryptocurrency transparency and institutionalizing block chain accountability.

Innovations offer dramatic improvements in system efficiencies that overcome resource demands currently constraining cryptocurrencies from global scale. As individuals and institutions are compensated for revealing intent, their participation enhances the attractiveness for others to enter markets with verifiable assets. These efficiency improvements are crucial, since this whole process will generate petabytes or even zettabytes of new data making it immensely costly to fish out the value of one or another data or meta data element.

Through rationalizing secure, reliable cryptocurrency and block chain transactions, these replicable processes and procedures reduce costs, accelerate speed, expedite verification and assure transparency. Proof of cryptocurrency value can then supplement and supersede proof of work. These systemic achievements achieve decentralization, security and scalability.

A Living Contract™, the foundational cornerstone of the paradigm, allows an individual, enterprise or institution to access permissioned data – that is data and meta data for which another individual, enterprise or institution authorizes access and acceptance – from multiple sources. "With these structures and guarantees, individuals, enterprises and institutions can securely transact the value of their data and metadata as they wish, with whom they wish, when they wish. Every data capture of a risk element in a living contract is preserved in its own unique light, so its transparency takes on value," Michael Harold, KNOWN™ Founder and Chief Technology Officer points out.

By affording intent, the Known Paradigm realizes transparency. "When looking at any population, there are two polarities which define the dialectic of intent," Harold points out. " At one terminal, we have the idea of transparency of information. It is provable that, given a global regime (political, regulatory, social, economic, etc.) that is supportive of transparency, increasing transparency increases value for the majority of direct participants in any and all participating social institutions. At the other terminal, we have the idea of obfuscation. If a given global regime is supportive of obfuscation, increasing obfuscation also increases value for the majority of direct participants in those same institutions. In one case (transparency), the benefit accrues to an increasingly larger heterogeneous population of direct participants. In the other case, the benefit accrues to an increasingly smaller, less heterogeneous population of direct participants."

Harnessing transparency with intent yields generational wealth creation. By rewarding intent, "digital dignity" superannuates "digital dispossession." Empowered with "digital dignity," individuals, enterprises and institutions have greater capacities to engage credit worthiness and artificial intelligence, key determinants of social and economic participation in 21st century society.[32]

Known Paradigm innovations are straightforward.

Clarifications of permissioned data and meta data quality indicate the monetary and risk values of any specific transaction at any point in time from origination through maturity. The higher the transparency of any specific revelation or disclosure, the greater the clarity and less the uncertainty reaching a decision to participate in a transaction. Parties and counterparties jointly and individually benefit from information symmetries for each's and all's rational calculations. These efficacies and efficiencies animate successive, not single instance or single industry, scaling and logarithmic growth for individual, enterprise and institution wealth creation at no marginal cost.

State of the art transactions-per-second speeds refine and reliably measure data quality to add value and to cut costs well beyond any growth in a wall garden or network elements in telecommunications networks.[33]

If one were to embrace the metaphor of a 21st century motor vehicle, top speed distributed ledger networks power engines. Living contracts provide lights, windshield windows, and steering for future, present and documented navigation. Data frames, data incentives and data marketplaces act as body, drive train and transmission. Bit coins and block chains serve as wheels.

All refine data and meta data to ground the 21st century gold standard by verifying transparent wealth and trustworthiness.

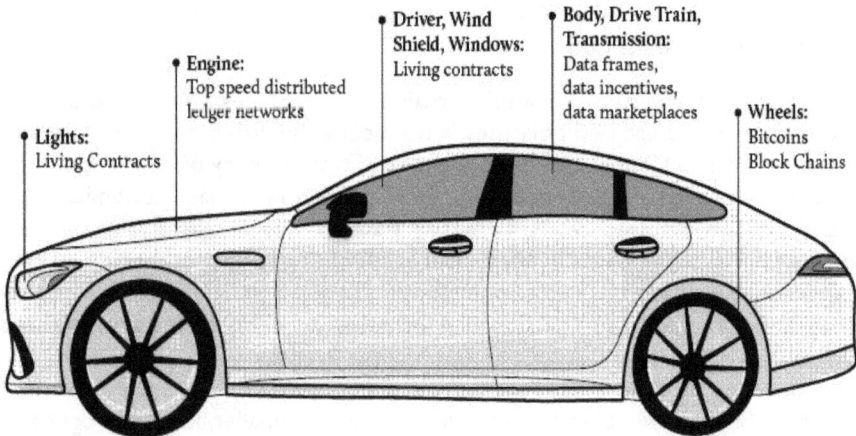

- Driver, Wind Shield, Windows: Living contracts
- Body, Drive Train, Transmission: Data frames, data incentives, data marketplaces
- Engine: Top speed distributed ledger networks
- Lights: Living Contracts
- Wheels: Bitcoins Block Chains

By adopting the paradigm, individuals, enterprises and institutions would create wealth for themselves instead of remaining passive users whose data and meta data create wealth for advertising paradigm incumbents. "Life only avails; not having lived. Power ceases in the instant of repose; it resides in the moment of transition from a past to a new state….," Ralph Waldo Emerson observed. Each and every individual, enterprise and institution transition from a 'user' to a creator of wealth for him, her and itself. Their data and meta data become alive. Individuals, enterprises and institutions elect how they wish to navigate and power themselves to destinations through oceans teeming with data and meta data.

It all makes sense historically.

In 1948, Claude Shannon memorably articulated *The Mathematical Theory of Communication*.[34] Shannon defined a paradigm for computer data efficacy and efficiency by classifying and typifying source, transmitter, channel, receiver and destination. His paradigm provided technologists, investors and adopters with widely accepted standards for developing and evaluating repeatable trial and error creating data networks. His achievement rationalized mainframe computing. As distributed computing emerged, it became as possible to measure search outcomes and to monetize relevance once browsers and search engines came into wide adoption.

In 1965, Gordon Moore[35] foresaw the doubling of microchip transistors every two years and the halving of computer prices.

In the 18th and 19th centuries, Adam Smith, David Ricardo and Karl Marx, among others, created classical economics and its criticism contesting the relative and absolute importance of labor as a component or theory of value.

Constance and Michael Erlanger and Michael Harold now articulate an information theory of value by measuring the risk and monetary values of individual, enterprise and institution revelations or disclosures of intent to transact data and meta data over distributed networks. The Known Paradigm renders the consequences[36] of the probabilities of classifying, typifying and monetizing data and meta data. As Ronald A. Howard observed his assessment of probabilistic and economic factors animated by Shannon's paradigm, "placing a value on the reduction of uncertainty is the first step in experimental design, for only when we know what it is worth to reduce uncertainty do we have a basis for allocating our resources in experimentation designed to reduce the uncertainty."[37]

By replacing uncertainty with transparency, the Erlangers and Michael Harold create standards enabling technologists, investors and adopters to measure distributed network data monetization through replicable trial and error.

Information Theory of Value

$$\text{Value of information} = \frac{(\text{Quantity of permissioned data \& meta data}^N)^N}{\text{Quality of permissioned data \& meta data}^N)^N}$$

$$= ((\text{Risk and monetary value }^N))^N$$

The dividend contains the quantities of data and meta data individuals, institutions and enterprises reveal or disclose.

The divisor measures its quality.

The quotient expresses the risk and monetary values of permissioned data and meta data.

Successive ^{Ns} in superscripts ^{N} depict growth.

With successive revelations or disclosures of individual, enterprise and institution intent to monetize data and meta data, all three elements (quantity, quality, measurement) scale network effects logarithmically. Internet and broadband mass production results through fresh individual, enterprise and institution capabilities to own, control, buy and sell data and meta data. Each and every revelation or disclosure creates more and greater value.

The Information Theory of Value resonates with mass production and reciprocity. "Mass production," as Paul W. Litchfield, longtime head of Goodyear Tire & Rubber remarks, "is more than labor-saving machinery and methods, more than substituting conveyor belts for wheelbarrows and men's backs, although that is part of it. It is more than breaking a job down into various parts so that each workman can become expert on his job, as against his making, more slowly, all the parts of a given product. That too is part of it. Reduced to simple terms, mass production seeks through every possible way to increase the productivity of the individual worker and to reduce the unit costs of the goods – and to pay men in proportion to what they produce, so encourage maximum output….In round numbers, wages in our plant went from about a dollar a day in 1900 to almost a dollar an hour as early as 1920."[38]

The Information Theory of Value applies this mass production orientation to data and meta data and achieves the highest productivity and greatest egalitarian wealth creation by reciprocating individual, enterprise and institution data and meta data wealth buying and selling data and meta data on self-selecting terms and conditions.

"Data value results from the continuous interplay of *choice and means*," Harold explains. "That is what KNOWN is proving: the value of choice or intent and means or opportunity as it applies to data. Whether that data is perceived as an attribute or measurement in time of a particular thing (what we generally refer to as reality) or as a means to create new data and things does not change the result. Intent (i.e., choice) and means (opportunity) are the basis of all data value.

Large tech corporations have taken away our choice and monopolized our means. This has to be reversed and a balance restored if this century is to retain any semblance of hope and opportunity for the majority of those who have yet to be born," he clarifies. If one were to embrace an architectural metaphor, the Known Paradigm organizes and refines site, light and gravity.[39] Individuals, enterprises and institutions embody sites. Intent (choice), opportunity (means) and data quality illuminate. Risk and monetary values ground. Everything is elemental. All refine data and meta data to ground the 21st

century gold standard by verifying transparent wealth and trustworthiness.

Known architecture elements

Site	Individual, enterprise and institution
Light	Intent (choice), opportunity (means) & Data Quality
Gravity	Risk and Monetary Values

These vibrancies incent individual, enterprise and institution to discard current Internet advertising paradigm trade-offs of surrendering privacy for access and efficiency. While advertising paradigm data and meta data increase in volume, they grow only each time an individual, enterprise and institution searches, and they only express value at instances where relevance of search outcomes yields advertising placement. In fact, the advertising paradigm appears to be more robust than it is or can be. Hence, the single ^{N} in the superscript ^{N} depicting growth.

Advertising Paradigm
(Quantity of Data and Meta Data)^N

Advertising paradigm incumbents and Internet advertising enterprises mine outcomes of individual, enterprise and institution searches to measure relevance for advertising placements. Generating revenue principally for inducing, stimulating, managing and fulfilling consumption is the central economic strength and weakness of relevance and the advertising paradigm. As soon as an advertising paradigm incumbent or spot market advertising placement enterprise has identified an individual, enterprise or institution as a likely target for one or another advertisement, advertisements appear on displays and mobile devices. All are inert and passive in clouds and oceans of data except for advertising paradigm incumbent cultivation and exploitation.

Privacy breaches, personal information theft, fraud and propaganda are but symptoms of relevance and advertising paradigm infirmities and negative externalities.

By contrast, the Known Paradigm embodies the brains and central nervous system of 21st century commerce. In these ways, the paradigm scales and extends late 20th century efficient market[40] conceptualizations and analysis to 21st century commerce. Due to transparency, Pareto optimality requiring mandatory transaction winner and loser can fade away as any transaction is a matter of acceptance or demurral based on its risk and monetary value indicated transparently in real time and near real time.

Data pipelines are the central nervous systems. KNOWN data pipelines as a service (DPaaS) afford secure, automated, scalable, cost and energy efficient data and meta data origination through maturity. Robust DPaaS capabilities power permissioned and tracked data and meta data. They spawn new, transparent lines of business. Incumbent intellectual property and software management regimes remain undisturbed.

Innovations establish egalitarian foundations for 21st century wealth creation and address seemingly intractable equity and sustainability issues bedeviling past and present.

FOR INDIVIDUAL LIBERTIES: Known Paradigm capabilities enable individuals, enterprises and institutions to permission uses of their health data and meta data as information and biological technologies become increasingly integrated and pervasive in society.

Paradigm capabilities exert countervailing individual, enterprise and institution freedom addressing proposed New IP authentication[41], which centralizes control and arbitrary censorship.[42]

They sustain individual, enterprise and institution freedoms as centralization and oligopoly[43] loom addressing the coronavirus and other vaccines.[44]

As consequentially, paradigm efficiencies and efficacies create viable markets and exchanges sustaining individual, enterprise and institution autonomy and decision making to countervail centralized, artificial-intelligence-powered automatons deploying facial recognition, retina scan and other surveillance technologies powering 21st century Internet oligopolies.

FOR ADVERTISERS: Advertisers could curtail advertising fraud losses[45] and more accurately track expenditures (e.g., "15% of advertiser spend",[46] an 'unknown delta,' representing around one-third of supply chain costs – could not be attributed," the ISBA[47] reported in the United Kingdom in May, 2020).

As cookies fade out, advertisers would wisely tap intent to enhance brand identities[48] within a comprehensive paradigm yielding real time and near real time market moving information for their clients.

FOR ASSET MANAGEMENT: The paradigm advances client best interest effecting prudent diversification management of the quality and quantity of pension fund assets, a timely contribution as hedge funds emerge more consequentially as managers in regulatory regimes implementing early-90's market administration.

FOR BANKING: Challenger banks could pick up innumerable new customers with Known transparency, incentives and rewards. The great burdens of the large incumbents are wide-spread conviction that they are "saddled with legacy tech and branch infrastructure, oversupply… and too little differentiation, offer[ing] unattractive rates and too many fees [and] lack...trust," FT Partners[49] pointed out in January, 2020. Customers are also increasingly amenable to contactless, electronic communications. Known Paradigm capabilities smooth the latter to address the former.

Capabilities also effect real time payments[50] between banks of all sizes, expedite liquidity coverage ratio[51] transactions, compliance and provide invaluable incentives to nonbank payment service providers to achieve network effects with cashless payments.

As importantly, banks acquire powerful tools to address the dominion of software and operating system contractors and providers.

Let's consider a world in which prevailing Internet and financial services are liberated .
Let's refer to this, in part, as competitive interactive computer services.

FOR CRYPTOCURRENCIES AND BLOCK CHAINS: Innovations measure and score value to ground and scale long term adoption as currencies and/or commodities.

FOR CLOUD COMPUTING: Innovations achieve multi-vendor, multi-functionality cloud presence, set cloud service standards and practices, manage costs, determine vendor selection and exit, clarify service agreement elements and components, and offer agility in contracting and managing cloud services. They assure privacy and security. Vulnerabilities like exposure of personal information for 80 million US households in an unprotected cloud database[52] would end. They make it cheaper and easier to comply with regulatory obligations.

FOR DOMINANT INCUMBENTS: Innovations make it possible for firms in search (Alphabet/Google), mobile communications and media (Apple), on-line retail (Amazon), social media (Facebook), cloud storage and computing (Amazon, Microsoft and others) and entertainment (Netflix) as well as network operators and any competitors emerging in their lines of business to grow and prosper in, with and through democratic markets in the 21st century; that is, to scale beyond relevance and to curtail security costs.

Alphabet, Amazon, Apple, Facebook, Microsoft and Netflix as well as network operators will be able to leverage newly permissioned information now fallow and unused as sources of additional income supplementing current profits.

As consequentially, dominant incumbent can pivot to compensated data and meta data. So doing will undo many advertising paradigm costs, notably in connection with security. But, the larger benefits inuring to dominant incumbents are insulation and inoculation from tort liabilities for claims of defamation. By migrating liability for defamation to the individuals, enterprises and institutions patronizing their platforms as Section 230 liability shield protections come under increasing scrutiny, dominant incumbents would be able to burden shift liability.

FOR MORE INCLUSIVE ECONOMIC EQUALITY: Paradigm digital
currencies enable narrowly tailored, precisely focused data and meta data markets enabling people of color, their white allies and impoverished rural Caucasians and their allies to direct wealth creation.

Alexis Ohanian, reddit co-founder, resigned from its board in June, 2020 amid national unrest and requested that the board contemplate an African American replacement. For Americans who share Ohanian's commitment to equality, yet do not command his wealth, Known Paradigm utilities enable wide participation to achieve economic equality and to remediate historic injustices.

The Known Paradigm rewards intentionality, the cornerstone for locally targeted investment breathing fresh life into impoverished regions, neighborhoods and communities, to scale wealth creation.

Specific elements, analogous to upvoting, can be adopted to scale urban black and rural poor white wealth. By defining precisely targeted areas and initiatives, transparency stimulates investment, equity and business diversity.

The paradigm's holistic approach affords the largest, sustainable wealth creation for urban blacks and rural, poor whites. For instance, after civil unrest, looting, arson, toppling of statues in many communities, Gallup found that 19%, just under 1 in 5 Americans, acknowledged race relations as America's "most important problem" in June, 2020.

"The historical record predicts that race will eventually fall back into its latent status, scoring relatively few mentions as a top-of-mind issue," Gallup observed. "The less top of mind race is as a major problem, presumably, the less likely politicians are going to feel pressure to take action.... [L]eaders are going to need to turn to other courses of action. One such strategy is to propose specific, tangible remedies…

Developing proposals to change existing attitudes in the ways that non-black Americans look at the race situation and to address the general concept of "systemic discrimination" in American culture and society will present more of a challenge."

By contrast, the Known Paradigm is sustainable. It creates virtuous cycles of investment. It rewards participants with fresh wealth for data and meta data they create investing in communities of their choosing.

FOR ENERGY: Efficiencies and efficacies expedite wholesale trading and accelerate widespread distributed generation markets.

FOR ENTERTAINMENT: Innovations turbo-charge immersive content production and consumption. Intent 'de-risks'[53] entertainment production and distribution by clarifying uncertainties regarding production investment and distribution costs with real and near real time data and meta data memorializing consumer intent. By engaging intent as predictive analytics, entertainment and production companies achieve greater control over capital costs, clearer forecasts of return on investment, and fewer surprises managing marketing costs.

FOR FAMILIES: Families would increase family wealth with Known Paradigm digital currencies transacting family member data and meta data.

FOR FINANCE: An exchange for blockchain commodities and currencies can be established and up and running.

Secondary markets can flourish and clear. KNOWN living contracts clarify monetary and asset risks for digital currency intermediaries and for exchange traded funds custom basket[54] construction and acceptance.

Capabilities enable transparent cryptocurrencies to rationalize scalable, decentralized transactions at higher speeds with greater security across block chains and siloed systems for accounting and monitoring efficiencies[55] and to achieve retail retention at lower transaction costs. With incumbent technologies alone, $300T globally, $100T USA and $10T in mortgage backed securities in the USA are in play.

KNOWN living contracts provide internal records for digital currency intermediaries and for exchange traded funds custom basket construction and acceptance.

FOR 5G WIRELESS, OPTICAL FIBER AND HYBRID FIBER COAXIAL WIRELINE COMMUNICATIONS, AND THE INTERNET OF THINGS: Functionalities create industry peace by rationalizing transparency, authentication and trust across exponentially more sources of data and meta data.

FOR HIGHLY FRACTURED MANUFACTURING AND SERVICE INDUSTRIES: Known Paradigm polyhedron architecture affords vertical efficiencies without vertical hierarchies.

FOR HIGHER EDUCATION: KNOWN living contracts address liability concerns coming out of the coronavirus pandemic.

FOR INSURANCE: Technologies recurrently update and clarify real time and near real time monetary and asset risks and values across many products and services including flood insurance.[56]

Known Paradigm capabilities expedite reopening the economy during the coronavirus pandemic through living contracts[TM] and immutable records to address tort liability.[57]

FOR INVESTORS AND SAVERS: Innovations map value and measure risk to provide confidence regarding cryptocurrency appreciation and depreciation over time and space.

FOR MACHINE LEARNING AND ARTIFICIAL INTELLIGENCE: Paradigm capabilities inflect investment in manufacturing, so crucial to reshoring supply chains.

FOR MORTGAGE SERVICERS AND LENDERS: Paradigm capabilities expedite CARES Act forbearance compliance.[58]

FOR NETWORK OPERATORS: Functionalities achieve retail retention at lower transaction costs.

FOR PUBLISHERS: The Known Paradigm creates currencies, contracts and records enabling publishers to vend content as they wish, to whom they wish, when they wish. Instead of a Hobson's Choice with one or another aggregator monopolist in search, social media or instant messaging, publishers can deploy Known digital currencies, living contracts,[TM] and immutable records for greater negotiation strength with interactive computer services as well as enabling publishers[59] to regain revenues now lost to advertising paradigm disintermediation. Intent incents opt-in[60] participation.

FOR SOCIAL INVESTING & ROBUST, INCLUSIVE ECONOMIC EQUALITY: The Known Paradigm rewards intentionality, the cornerstone for locally targeted investment breathing fresh life into impoverished regions, neighborhoods and communities, to scale wealth creation.

Paradigm digital currencies enable narrowly tailored, precisely focused data and meta data markets enabling people of color, their white allies and impoverished rural Caucasians and their allies to direct wealth creation.

Alexis Ohanian[61], reddit co-founder, resigned from its board in June, 2020 amid national unrest and requested that the board contemplate an African American replacement. For Americans who share Ohanian's commitment to equality, yet do not command his wealth, Known Paradigm utilities enable wide participation to achieve economic equality and to remediate historic injustices.

Specific elements, analogous to upvoting, can be adopted to scale urban black and rural poor white[62] wealth. By defining precisely targeted areas and initiatives, transparency stimulates investment, equity and business diversity.

The paradigm's holistic approach affords the largest, sustainable wealth creation for urban blacks and rural, poor whites. For instance, after civil unrest, looting, arson, toppling of statues in many communities, Gallup found that 19%, just under 1 in 5 Americans, acknowledged race relations as America's "most important problem" in June, 2020.

"The historical record predicts that race will eventually fall back into its latent status, scoring relatively few mentions as a top-of-mind issue," Gallup observed. "The less top of mind race is as a major problem, presumably, the less likely politicians are going to feel pressure to take action.... [L]eaders are going to need to turn to other courses of action. One such strategy is to propose specific, tangible remedies... Developing proposals to change existing attitudes in the ways that non-black Americans look at the race situation and to address the general concept of "systemic discrimination" in American culture and society will present more of a challenge.[63]

By contrast, the Known Paradigm is sustainable. It creates virtuous cycles of investment and commercial activity. It rewards participants with fresh wealth for data and meta data they create investing in and patronizing enterprises in communities of their choosing.

In other words, the Known Paradigm oxygenates individuals, enterprises and institutions, which have endured invidious discrimination. It invigorates with recurrent wealth. Hence, it is the opposite of a boycott. Boycotts asphyxiate by forestalling

income and revenue.

"As we embark on the creation of new information relationships involving new entrustees and new kinds of personal information, we must ensure that the essential elements of social trust are built into them so that our new relationships can be as sustainable as our older ones," Neil Richards and Woodrow Hartzog observe in a *Stanford Law Review*[64] article. "Trust is necessary for a sustainable digital future... create[ing] individual and social value."

Known Paradigm innovations afford trust and effect transparency by originating and rationalizing intent as a fresh network element.

This historically distinct achievement addresses 21st century technological innovation like artificial intelligence biotechnology and climate and ecological challenges with a paradigm evaluating repeatable trial and error creating wealth in these emerging fields.

Too often, solutions, initially tailored for industrial capitalism, apply remediations like anti-trust or sunshine regulation. While effective correcting a wrong doing once it has occurred, these fundamentally retrospective approaches are invariably palliative. Enterprise and innovation are always a step ahead.

These outcomes, in turn, spawn devolutionary assertions calling for greater discretion and control for corporations and individuals, but increased efficiency can often diminish consumer welfare, the environment and public health.

Or, the necessarily narrowly tailored scope of the reforms animates massive, beneficially intended solutions like single payer health or a guaranteed annual income addressing one or other symptom of wealth inequality.

By contrast, the Known Paradigm empowers any and everyone creating data and meta data to participate in creating wealth by doing so as each and all engage 21st century markets and society.

Chapter two examines the roles of relevance and the advertising paradigm shaping and defining the commercial Internet. By monopolizing data and meta data, dominant first movers retard scaling Internet and broadband mass production. Internal weaknesses and negative externalities so compromise relevance, advertising and the commercial Internet that relevance now deserves a rest.

Relevance Deserves A Rest

CHAPTER TWO

Relevance Deserves A Rest

For all their power, prestige and income, dominant incumbents are constraining their supremacy in the future by cultivating approaches that extended their hegemony in the past. Firms specializing in search (Alphabet/Google), mobile communications and media (Apple), on-line retail, home monitoring and cloud computing (Amazon), social media and online payment exchanges (Facebook), operating system, cloud computing and productivity (Microsoft) and entertainment (Netflix) remain substantially and, in some instances, exclusively focused on developing new technologies, services and markets extending lines of business to boost advertising revenues.

In the advertising paradigm, individuals, enterprises and institutions willingly trade precious amounts of privacy and personal information in return for efficiency and mobility. Participants give voluminous attention to Internet and mobile device amusement, convenience, diversion, efficacy and engagement. Dominant incumbents then place advertisements of relevance to individuals, enterprises and institutions on their devices and receive revenues for those placements. Network providers require subscriptions for access and speed. Entertainment providers offer subscriptions. Search and social media enterprises employ free data. All incumbents, in one way or another, pursue relevance to drive revenues.

Alphabet/Google, Amazon, Apple, Facebook, Microsoft and Netflix (often referred to, in part, as FAANG) are preserving and protecting implementations of relevance originating from mainframe computing over 70 years ago. "The summation of human experience is being expanded at a prodigious rate, and the means we use for threading through the consequent maze to the momentarily important item is the same as was used in the days of square-rigged ships," Vannevar Bush observed in *Endless Horizons* (1946). In 1960, *The Oxford English Dictionary* documented the initial computer science definition of relevance as "the basic problem of information retrieval is that of the relevance number, which provides a means of ranking documents according to their probable relevance." By the close of the twentieth century, the *OED* attested to the continued importance of relevance as follows: "Some search engines rank for relevance, but their measure of relevance might be just how many times your search word occurs in a document." In the middle of the first decade of the 21st century the *OED* stated that "Google... does measure relevance mostly in terms of incoming links, not newness." In 2003, Tableau began data visualization and may apply those capabilities to visualizing operations in real-time or near real-time. Increasing numbers of appliances (home thermostats), personal devices (smart phones, Fitbits) and artificial intelligence and machine learning algorithms (reinforcement learning) represent and express gambits to entrench monopoly or oligopoly positions.

Despite its legacy utility, relevance is two steps removed from intent. It's old from the get-go. Relevance indicates propinquity, proximity, and nearness in time, space and association to a separate act or instance at prior moments in time. According to *The Oxford English Dictionary*, relevance expresses "the property of fulfilling the requirements of a user's search for information; the degree to which a document, web page, etc., fulfils such requirements." While relevance embodies "pertinence to current or important issues, interests, needs, etc.; appositeness," (*OED*) an individual, enterprise or institution has already resolved intent beforehand by the moment in time any person, business or institution initiates a search, which relevance then measures. Relevance, therefore, is definitionally a measurement of a search, originated by prior intent, that is taking place or has transpired. While not exclusively retrospective, relevance preponderantly, though not exclusively, mines present and past to try to predict the future.

A search expresses intent. Without a prior desire, purpose, willed inclination or decision, either at that moment or beforehand, animating an inquiry, there is no search. Search remains inescapably a consequence and iteration of intent. Code and algorithms remove search from intent's origination and complexity to intermediate precision and appositeness.

Relevance measures search. When relevance scores or measures the outcome of a search, relevance strives to identify whether a search expresses an intent for future action or simply indicates a desire to satisfy a curiosity.

Relevance is twice burdened. As the basis for evaluating seemingly apposite responses to a search request, relevance approximates intent to the extent of its algorithm's explanatory power. Relevance and the advertising paradigm put the cart before the horse. They attempt to lead an individual, enterprise or institution by the nose to a consumption decision sponsored by an advertising patron (e.g., one or another eating establishment or accommodation along an itinerary). Relevance is engineered to reward an advertiser more than to fulfill individual, enterprise or institution intent. It is in this way that sales funnels are consequential.

These capabilities – measuring an outcome of a search to approximate intent – vindicate relevance's essential nature. Relevance is inherently and exclusively derivative. As such, relevance can never express originality, will, intention, pleasure or desire, intent's essential energy and elemental quality. At best, it can strive to capture some aspect of each. Inevitably, relevance's wholly derivative ontology devolves inescapably to abuse like psycho-political manipulation and parasitism like identity theft and credit card theft, so that, in the end, relevance animates voluminous costs attempting to secure commercially harvested data and meta data. It is in these senses that the commercial Internet is broken, and relevance deserves a rest.

Following collapse of the dot com bubble in 2000, Google pioneered relevance to generate advertising revenues to realize a fresh business model. By offering free search, individuals, enterprises and institutions flooded Google for information, willingly ceding privacy, for efficacy and efficiency. Google, the noun, morphed to a verb. One simply "googled" whatever he or she sought. Advertising obviated subscription fees. By mining and analyzing that search information, Google reaped staggering revenues by offering advertisers timely data for placements. Relevance's promoters and practitioners then plugged its indispensability to predict intent based on search analyses and analytics augmented with consumption histories and demographic data. The degree to which inflation characterized assertions presented through edge provider mattered little from any earlier marketing campaign in the nation's history from patent medicines to P.T. Barnum. All the action was at the edges, so Congress did nothing to interfere with a new goose and its golden eggs. No-Internet-tax and liability immunity law and regulation stimulated on-line retail and social media, subsequently. And, at the turn of the 21st century, commercial Internet promoters also expressed concerns that banner advertisements were too anemic to stimulate adequate revenues to scale a commercial Internet.

It was and remains a generational achievement for the commercial Internet and distributed networks. Google accomplished advertising placement efficiencies by transitioning point-to-multipoint broadcast commercial and newspaper display and classified advertising to multipoint-to-point distributed network and, eventually, mobile device display advertising. "In their capacities to hold effortless interest and their accessibility over the entire cultural spectrum, and their independence of any educational qualification, these were admirably suited to mass persuasion . ... Radio and more especially television have, in consequence, become the prime instruments for the management of consumer demand," John Kenneth Galbraith observed in *The New Industrial State* (1971). "The industrial system is profoundly dependent on commercial television and could not exist in its present form without it. Economists, who eschew discussion of its economic significance, or dismiss it as a wicked waste, are protecting their reputation and that of their subject for Calvinist austerity. But they are not adding to their reputation for relevance."

Advertising is the indispensable correlate. Advertising energizes and compensates for relevance's essential derivativeness measuring a search. By drawing one's attention to search complements and substitutes, advertising pays for free data for individuals, enterprises and institutions and reaps billions for Internet and broadband first movers.

Advertising originates from "Anglo-Norman and Middle French avertiss, advertiss…,[a] lengthened stem of *avertir, advertire*…. From an early date the ending was frequently either apprehended as or assimilated to -ize," *The Oxford English Dictionary* defines. Advertising calls or turns one's attention to one or another good, service or idea. Its most common sense meaning in 2020 is "to make generally known by means of an announcement in a public medium."[65]

Google's momentous attainment operationalizing Internet advertising created the advertising paradigm. As Thomas Kuhn, originator of "paradigm shift,"[66] points out, "to be accepted as a paradigm, a theory must seem better than its competitors, but it need not, and in fact never does, explain all the facts with which it can be confronted."[67] As the measurement standard for Internet and mobile device advertising placement, relevance powers for paradigm for the commercial Internet and distributed computing; the so called, edge services.

By way of analogy, relevance embodies Silicon Valley advertising innovation comparable to Michael Bloomberg's transformation of financial markets with electronic real-time yield curves in the early 1980's. Bloomberg information and data became the de facto standards for trader and investor decision making. Bloomberg terminals added news and private email services to position the firm as a critical, if not indispensable, financial services communications resource. In 2020, Forbes ranked Michael Bloomberg as the 15th wealthiest man in the world with real time net worth of $54.9B.[68]

Similarly, relevance has transformed comparison shopping. In 1983, The Cantor Fitzgerald financial services firm revolutionized the U.S. government securities market by pioneering screen-based trading. Cantor delivered real-time computer displays of the bid and offer prices and the fees available from multiple brokers, accompanied by a trade execution facility. What today looks like a rather primitive system based on proprietary monitors hardwired to a central computer introduced a form of comparative shopping that rendered existing trading methods, based on voice communications and facsimile confirmations, obsolete. In effect, Cantor introduced a network element by pioneering an electronic exchange in treasury bonds. His success attracted brokers to rent pages to display offerings and led to network effects for computer terminals as others entered electronic trading. Cantor's exchange promoted competition, which enhanced consumer welfare by spurring innovation and reducing transaction costs. Cantor's innovation helped the Treasury. Comparative monitor displays simplified risk matching: any broker or buyer using the terminal could match the risk tolerance of individual buyers to specific bonds (e.g., 10 years yielding 4%, or 20 years yielding 5%). Cantor's innovation also resolved time and space. A buyer like California Public Employees Retirement System (CalPERS) could see and undertake a trade on a price listed in New York in real time on the basis of current information and immediate execution. Neil Hirsch did initial design and commercialization with his firm Telerate in which Cantor had invested early on and whose functionalities he improved. This also increased demand for AT&T's long-distance lines for increased volumes of continuously updated data.

During the first two decades of the 21st century, relevance emerged as the *de facto* standard for Internet product and service advertising placement over distributed networks and mobile devices as individuals, enterprises and institutions initiated and compared one or another search outcome. Gross-to-granular relevance calculations of contemporaneous and historic search outcomes reaped billions of dollars in profits for dominant incumbents. See Appendix I. If an individual relies on Google Maps for itineraries and directions and places the itinerary on a mobile device, Google knows the journey. Furthermore, Google knows past search histories documenting interest in one or another matter. Amazon knows search and consumption information. Its web services platform expertly places inducements on individual devices based on search outcomes. Facebook learns whatever one member shares with another about an activity or issue, including the intention to engage in various activity at various locations at various times through its core service as well as through its WhatsApp and Instagram platforms. Most often, however, relevance proves to be an accurate indication of intent when an individual, enterprise or institution conducts a search to acquire information related to one or another product or service supplemented with other identifiable data on age, gender, financial condition, geographic location, organizational affiliation, social connection, etc.

Propinquity is an increasingly big deal with smart phones and tablets. Location, location, location – the cornerstone of real estate – grounds advertising placement for readiest consumption.

Shoshana Zuboff now introduces "surveillance capitalism" to define the commercial Internet as a historically specific mode of capital accumulation. In a consequential, ably argued essay,[69] published in connection with The Age of Surveillance Capitalism[70]

(2019), the Harvard Business School professor and scholar contends that Internet incumbents enforce an environment of "digital dispossession," impelling individuals, enterprises and institutions to surrender "decision rights" over their privacy. "Surveillance capitalism originates in this act of *digital dispossession*, operationalized in the *rendition* of human experience as behavioral data," she contends.

Surveillance capitalism, in so many words, obliterates the reciprocal relations undergirding industrial capitalism. Unlike 20th century manufacturers vending to consumers, surveillance capitalists flourish by selling the "behavioral surplus" of individual, enterprise and institution data and metadata "in new *behavioral futures* markets in which users are neither buyers nor sellers nor products. Instead, users are the human natural source of free raw material that feeds a new kind of manufacturing process designed to fabricate prediction products. These products are calculations that predict what individuals and groups will do now, soon, and later,"[71] Zuboff finds.

Note well: the products express inflation: they masquerade the future based on approximations of the past. In the most elemental sense, they are history, the past, predicting to define present and future.

Concerns over the social costs of surveillance capitalism are rising. "Now in the first decades of the twenty-first century the distinct social, political, and economic interests of "users" have yet to be carefully distinguished from the de facto conditions of experiential dispossession, datafication, control, and commodification introduced by surveillance capitalism, reified in its behavioral futures markets, and enforced by its unique and ever-widening instrumentarian power. Unless this latency is evoked into new forms of collective action, the trajectory of the digital future will be left to the new hegemon: surveillance capitalism and its unprecedented asymmetries of knowledge and power,"[72] Zuboff assesses.

As with any substantial, original work, Zuboff animates supplemental insights. For instance, Zuboff places 20th century scientific management in perspective.

Remarking on the emergence of scientific management, Paul W. Litchfield, President and CEO of Goodyear Tire & Rubber Company for a goodly portion the first half of the twentieth century, observes in Industrial Voyage My Life as an Industrial Lieutenant (1954): "The new type of business leadership came in. The captain of industry passed out of the picture. As Fortune magazine once phrased it: 'The present was as far as he could go.' He was succeeded by managers and administrators, men who sought to organize teamwork attack on the problem of large-scale production to match large-scale markets and to reconcile the various conflicts of interest among employees, stockholders, and consumers, and on a fairer basis than before, as men became increasingly conscious of underlying social and economic forces...."[73]

"The basic in that [scientific management] thinking was a recognition of the consumer as the man who paid all wages and provided all profits. Instead of charging him as much as the traffic would bear, American industry concluded that the immediate dollar was not too important, that it would be ahead in the long run if it built the maximum of value into its product and charged as little for it as it could. Greater value would make more people desire those goods, and the lower price would reach down into lower income brackets, and more people could afford to buy.... There were thousands of potential new customers a company might reach, if it could bring value up and price down.... The old idea was that whatever a company paid out in wages was subtracted from its profits, consequently it should work its men long hours and pay them as little as it had to. But now with the need for low-cost, large-volume production, it was good business to offer the incentive of good pay for the more efficient use of the new machines coming in. Wages were based on output rather than on hours spent at the workbench. The piece work system became an incentive to individual productivity. Wages went up and the workday grew shorter."[74]

"Then a surprising thing came to light, something I do not think many had anticipated. The employee became a customer, for his own and everyone's goods. Industry uncovered a wealth of potential customers under its own roof. Only in America do men drive to work in automobiles they themselves build. Well-paid work-men helped build up the nation's purchasing power... The system created a new market, and supplied it.... The plain people of America shared in the benefits. Living and working conditions improved more in this period than they had in all the years up to that time combined – and are vastly better than people know in any other part of the globe." (pages 21-22)

Frederick Winslow Taylor's scientific management rationalized 19th century craft methods to achieve 20th century industrial efficiency and productivity. This undergirds industrial employment reciprocity. "...[W]henever a workman proposes an improvement, it should be the policy of the management to make a careful analysis of the new method, and if necessary conduct a series of experiments to determine accurately the relative merit of the new suggestion and of the old standard. And whenever the new method is found to be markedly superior to the old, it should be adopted as the standard for the whole establishment. The workman should be given the full credit for the improvement, and should be paid a cash premium as a reward for his ingenuity. In this way the true initiative of the workmen is better attained under scientific management than under the old, [craft] individual plan,"[75] Taylor recommended.

None of this egalitarian wealth creation, undergirded by reciprocity, transpires with the advertising paradigm and digital dispossession in the commercial Internet. By widely welcoming diverse participation, dominant Internet incumbents acquire wealth by extracting value from Internet data and meta data, and, consequently, they do not need their employees to be their customers to achieve wealth as was the case with industrial capitalism. Manufacturing wealth, as Litchfield details[76], Taylor architects and Zuboff casts in bright contrasting light, impelled reciprocity and in the process effected egalitarian wealth creation.

Litchfield is exact about reciprocity in industrial capitalism: "Cars built so inexpensively under mass production that millions of people could afford them created jobs for an army of men in the automobile plants and those producing spark plugs, electric starters, tires, and all the rest; jobs as well in steel, rubber, leather, glass, aluminum, and other industries; for men driving cars and trucks, selling them, servicing them, repairing them, refueling them, for men building highways and working in warehouses. Thousands of new technical, engineering, chemical, accounting, scheduling, and administrative jobs came in which did not exist before –

not to count the opportunities created for men to go into business for themselves as dealers in cars, tires, gasoline, accessories – or operator of roadside hotels. All of which appears to me a better way of sharing the wealth – i.e., give a large number of people the chance to earn money for themselves..."[77]

By contrast, the advertising paradigm and relevance power hoarding[78] and income and wealth inequality[79] by extracting the 'behavioral surplus' as well as the advertising placement value of individual, enterprise and institution transactions.

Note well that luck, entrepreneurship and astute real estate investment[80] contribute crucially to wealth creation in industrial capitalism no less than the commercial Internet powered by relevance animating advertising revenues.

Zuboff's periodization of surveillance capitalism allows readers to grasp Internet and broadband wireless and wireline communications and markets with greater perspective, acuity and precision. For example, her approach contributes to behavioral psychology by placing Edward Bernays's achievements with publicity to inflect consumption of tobacco, bacon and eggs, among other products, in historic perspective.

Network security emerges as the source of substantial additional costs. Security has to be in place to fend off hackers and thieves; that is, gaining "unauthorized access to or control over" (OED) digitally dispossessed data and metadata. Zuboff discusses security principally as further surveillance intrusion in home monitoring, heating and air conditioning.

Self-identified "ethical" or "white hat hackers"[81] are now emerging to secure bounties by detecting data weaknesses for the largest enterprises. Hacker training and employment platforms offer hacker education and employment opportunities. What is unambiguous in each instance, whether black hat extortion or white hat remediation, is that the porousness of network security undergirds their existence.

Insights animated by Zuboff are surgical. Hacking is the as illegal complement to extraction and rendition. Data misuse, misappropriation and privacy violations are inescapable exploitations of the advertising paradigm of data extraction and rendition.

The permeability of network security exposes the Internet's Achilles Heel, George Gilder[83] observes. His language is gentlemanly. Advertising paradigm infirmities express 'security' failures through breakdowns managing voluminous data and meta data.

But for security, data extraction and metadata rendition would become so grossly compromised that individuals, enterprises and institutions would seek substitutes to dominant Internet monopolists and oligopolists. Mergers and acquisitions[84] and market consolidation[85] in artificial intelligence and machine learning security systems typify industry needs.

Real time bidding spot markets give fresh relevance paradigm expression to the Wild West. As Johnny Ryan, Brave Chief Policy and Industry Relations Officer reported of the United Kingdom Information Commission report on real time bidding: "As bid requests are often not sent to single entities or defined groups of entities, the potential is for these requests to be processed by any organization using the available protocols, whether or not they are on any vendor list and whether or not they are processing personal data in accordance with the requirements of data protection law.... Multiple parties receive information about a user, but only one will 'win' the auction to serve that user an advert. There are no guarantees or technical controls about the processing of personal data by other parties, e.g., retention, security etc. In essence, once data is out of the hands of one party, essentially that party has no way to guarantee that the data will remain subject to appropriate protection and controls."[86] Facebook litigation with Rankwave[87] attests to the infirmities. Facebook's tightening up of application program interfaces (APIs)[88] was comparably revealing.

Misappropriation of personal data and metadata – 87 million in Facebook's case providing "intimate emotional-based data to Cambridge Analytica[89] to manipulate voting behavior" as psychologist Frederick Lowen observed of the 2016 presidential election -- exemplifies failures, negative externalities and anomalies inescapable in the advertising paradigm.

"The owners of the platforms that created the algorithms are at a loss," Renee DiResta remarks in a thoughtful commentary exploring computational propaganda in The Yale Review. "They struggle to define their responsibilities, they struggle with the subtle distinctions among propaganda, disinformation, and misinformation, and they struggle with a desire to remain neutral and maintain a commitment to the principle of free speech. The decision of whether and how to moderate content is complex; First Amendment protections don't apply to users who post content on a private platform, and legally the platforms have their own First Amendment right to moderate content.[90]

The Federal Trade Commission announced a consent order and imposed a $5B fine in July, 2019. "Facebook agreed to an order that...1) prohibited Facebook from making misrepresentations about the privacy or security of consumers' information, 2) prohibited Facebook from misrepresenting the extent to which it shares personal data, and 3) required Facebook to implement a reasonable privacy program....The...penalty is the largest ever imposed on any company for violating consumers' privacy and almost 20 times greater than the largest privacy or data security penalty ever imposed worldwide,"

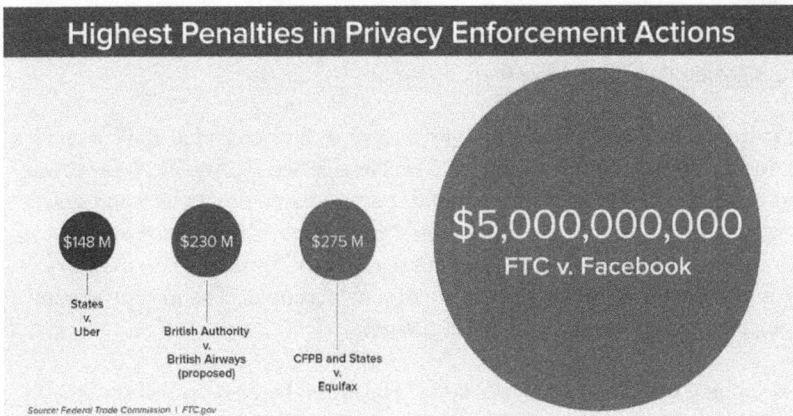

the FTC indicated.

Highest Penalties in Privacy Enforcement Actions

$148 M

States v. Uber

$230 M

British Authority v. British Airways (proposed)

$275 M

CFPB and States v. Equifax

$5,000,000,000

FTC v. Facebook

Source: Federal Trade Commission | FTC.gov

Facebook had disregarded a 2012 Federal Trade Commission consent order[92] and found itself in the hotseat following the 2016 presidential election. A 2019 consent decree requires privacy monitoring. Regulators touted privacy violation remediations and preventions, and they are advocating for fresh authority[93] to extract civil penalties for first offenses and to regulate non-profits and common carriers.

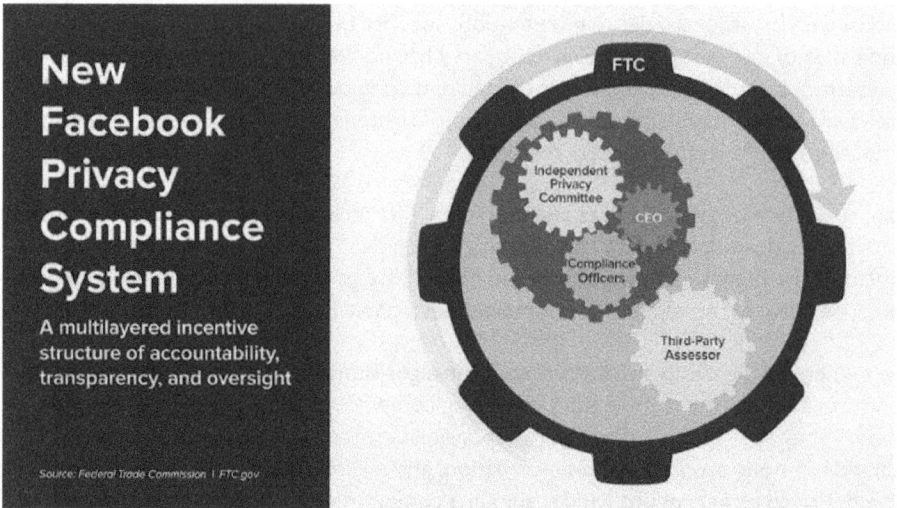

New Facebook Privacy Compliance System

A multilayered incentive structure of accountability, transparency, and oversight

Source: Federal Trade Commission | FTC.gov

The Department of Justice will initiate civil litigation seeking civil penalties for alleged Facebook violations of its 2012 consent decree with the FTC regarding privacy, the FTC indicated at the time.[94]

Such regulatory solutions draw attention to the scope of Progressive public policy to address 21st century abuses. Policing wrongdoing after it has been proven to have occurred yields prospective accommodations with tardy corrections leaving the advertising paradigm undisturbed but for acknowledged, unlawful activity. Litigation against One Audience[95] concerning a software development kit[96] improperly scraping private information, initiated in February, 2020, attested to compliance with the fresh decree and order. The corrections may well curtail third party abuses going forward. Certainly, it is in Facebook's interest to stop such parasitism following the fresh order and decree. If anything, fine memorialized 'move fast and break things' Facebook youth and monitoring signaled late teen adolescence.

Facebook was maturing to young adulthood with shopping, finance and digital currencies and putting its adolescence behind with the 2019 consent order. In May, 2019, Facebook announced that it will be cultivating point-to-point, person-to-person buying and selling through its digital marketplace and that it will aggregate groups "that emblematize… identity,"[97] news reports indicated. The latter centralizes event[98] planning and memory, a rich data trove for vending advertising for recurrent celebrations. The former admits wider advertising placement vehicles and opportunities.

Within a week, tapping political speech policies,[99] Facebook banned Louis Farrakhan,

Alex Jones, Laura Loomer, Paul Nehlen, Paul Joseph Watson and Milo Yiannopoulos as part of a broader initiative ostensibly policing hate speech[100]. To the extent FTC settlement terms may have triggered the bans, provocative free speech issues arise in connection with private censorship. Coming ahead of publication of a fresh consent order and news of a fine, the gestures won prestige press approbation.

The same is true with fraud. Any alert reader could readily infer that fraud expresses the illegal complement to legally permitted digital dispossession.

Behavior expresses another facet. Social adoption of binary, yes or no thinking and ideation is one of the great, pervasive-so-widely-accepted-incessantly-reiterated-unquestioningly-adopted-that-it-is-taken-for-granted-and-hence-almost-always-invisible artifacts of relevance and the advertising paradigm. Decision making[101] is emerging more forcefully as consciousness. As individuals are growing increasingly accustomed to recurrent yes or no thinking, such ideation is ideal for sales funnels. Once an individual, enterprise or institution reaches one or another binary choice it is then a matter of defining more and other choices to inflect and trigger adoption of a product, service, good, candidate, idea or ideology.

Cultivation and exploitation of such pervasively adopted binary, yes or no decision making is now a multi-billion- dollar business implicating trillions of dollars of assets.

Virtually all the cultivation and exploitation are narrowly opportunistic and self-serving in the senses that competent cultivation and exploitation practitioners thrive only to the extents they feed on and off individual, enterprise and institution behavioral surpluses, in Zuboff's turn of phrase, harvested by relevance and the advertising paradigm.

In these ways, the initial symbiosis of search and of social media, pioneered respectively by Google in 2000 and Facebook in 2004, morphed to self-serving opportunism and commercial, some would say, parasitic exploitation. Attention engineering[102] cultivated addictive behavior crowding out efficiency and efficacy. The commercial Internet may well be contributing to the triggering of anger[103] among many individuals, enterprises and institutions twenty years later.

Manipulation of binary choice, yes or no decision making sooner or later tires leaving many feeling patronized and resentful confined to no choice but to respond repeatedly to what an algorithm indicates he or she intends with the sole purpose of inflecting a consumption decision the individual, enterprise or institution may find the least worst of possible choices. A great deal of the process is not Hobson and is often maddening. This *sui generis* relevance and advertising paradigm manipulation of individual, enterprise and institution decision making[104] may well be contributing to dysphoria, dissatisfaction and restlessness as binary, yes or no ideation pervades consciousness regarding ideas, journalism, public policy, political candidates and national and international institutions.

In tucking it to brick and mortar establishments and municipal tax bases, the commercial Internet early on attested to Americans' love affair with selective law enforcement. Armed with federal protections encouraging a baby industry, federal law afforded liability immunities and local sales tax forgiveness, each and both indispensable to logarithmic scaling of the commercial Internet, relevance and the advertising paradigm shuttering many a mom-and-pop business and savaging municipal business tax revenues in the process. All legal as an impelling digital correlate to James Thurlow Adam's telling frontier insight: "One other element may be taken into consideration, the effect of the frontier," Adams observed in 1928. "Until thirty years ago, America has always had a frontier, and that fact has been of prime importance in many respects for the national outlook. For our purpose we may merely note that in the rough life of the border there is scant recognition for law as law. Frequently remote from the courts and authority of the established communities left behind, the frontiersman not only has to enforce his own law, but he elected what laws he shall enforce and what he shall cease to observe. Payment of debt, especially to the older settlements, may come to be looked upon lightly, whereas horse stealing may be punishable with shooting at sight." So, with digital commerce, relevance and the advertising paradigm in the gold rush for digital attention and intimate behavioral information.

Vance Packard, Galbraith's contemporary and correlate for advertising, anticipated these dysphoric outcomes in The Hidden Persuaders (1957) arguing that advertisers manipulate desire and longing and The Naked Society (1964), an early alert on data privacy.

All these developments affirm Zuboff's acuity. Her achievement creates fresh perspectives on individual, enterprise and institution behavior creating meaning and value with contemporary Internet and broadband communications within the advertising paradigm.

This is, in a very real sense, "where the rubber hits the road" because relevance and the advertising paradigm could not thrive as fully as they do without affording benefits. For investors, exchanges and major banks overseeing initial public offerings, relevance and the advertising paradigm have been lucrative particularly for investors, who bet on dominant incumbents. Individuals, enterprises and institutions access search and social media functionalities voluntarily at no cost. Private individuals could rent accommodation in their home or offer transportation with their vehicles through aggregator contractors like Airbnb, Uber and Lyft. Such so-called sharing services sustained many persons following the 2008 asset crisis enabling many to keep their homes and others to acquire income. As mass market consumers, individuals, enterprises and institutions exercise consumption decisions. They govern amenability, susceptibility and surrender fully as much as indifference and imperviousness to sales funnels. Professional, salaried and wage workers often earn income physically removed from a workplace. Wide varieties of individually and family owned enterprises creating and vending creative, small batch products from music to beverages to garments and well beyond could and do reach suppliers and buyers with the efficiency of the Internet and broadband networks.

For dominant incumbents, advertising placement firms and advertisers, relevance and the advertising paradigm yield lots of benefits and restrain with golden chains. Their vast fortunes depend on carrying both forward in existing and new lines of business to address market valuation, market capitalization and competition. Microsoft thrives with web development tool kits, and Amazon soars with web services. Probabilities that searches are generally, but not precisely, exact boost recurrent advertiser web placement service patronage. Web developers seek competitive advantage for salaries[105] with technical proficiencies employing C#, Clojure[106], Elixir, Go, Kolton, Microsoft TypeScript, Kotlin, Python, Rust, Swift and Web Assembly languages. These professional incentives and business practices protract relevance and advertising paradigm inefficiencies.

JavaScript extended and scaled relevance and the advertising paradigm. In many ways, JavaScript analogizes to the Ford Motor Car Company Model A[107]. Or, if one were to embrace a General Motors analogy, JavaScript is metaphorically akin to the electrical starter motor, octane efficiency and output (methylcyclopentadienyl manganese tricarbonyl) in leaded and unleaded gasoline, and lacquers enabling color paints in automotive vehicles pioneered by Charles Franklin Kettering, Alfred P. Sloan's collaborator and partner. "[A] generation of browser implementors, engine developers, framework designers, standards contributors, tool builders, and Web application programmers found pragmatic ways to use and enhance JavaScript, usually without breaking the Web," Allen Wirfs-Brock and Brendan Eich[108] observed in June, 2020.

The great bet is whether and how fully the use of "relevance" and the advertising paradigm can and will be imposed on present and future.

It is not a big stretch to think of the dominant Internet incumbents and network operators as electronic and digital correlates of twentieth century monopolists and oligopolists:

Alphabet/ Google	The Encyclopedia Britannica, the Associated Press
Amazon	Sears Roebuck and the Bell System
Apple	National Cash Register, EMI, CBS, BMG, PolyGram, WEA and MCA records and the Bell System
Facebook	International, national and local newspapers
Microsoft	IBM, the Bell System and Western Union
Netflix	Paramount Pictures, Warner Bros. Pictures, Universal Pictures, Columbia Pictures, Walt Disney Studios, Metro-Goldwyn-Mayer and RKO

None is fated to perpetuity any more than their 19th and 20th century correlates. In many ways, the market power of dominant Internet incumbents is more vulnerable to substitution. Nineteenth and twentieth century monopolies and oligopolies consolidated market power by controlling physical assets like ire ore, coal, oil, copper and transportation facilities and networks. One need only think of Carnegie tying up Mesabi Iron Range ore, Rockefeller refining oil, or William A. Clark, Marcus Daly and

F. Augustus Heinze dominating copper mining. All any new Internet and digital currency entrant needs to do today is develop something jazzier and more secure using network elements that are distinctly more pliant and readily available than physical elements.

For instance, the dominant interactive computer service first movers, Alphabet/Google, Facebook and Twitter achieve market power through monopolizing wholesale data and meta data markets principally, but not exclusively, for spot market advertisers.

By contrast, the Known Paradigm enables robust individual, enterprise and institution data and meta data retail markets to emerge, thrive and multiply, (i.e., "the action or business of selling goods in relatively small quantities for use or consumption rather than for resale," *OED*).

The most pertinent industrial analogy may well be Ford Motor Company's Model T. Henry Ford achieved market dominance transforming horse drawn carriages by adding an internal combustion engine, radiator, transmission, steering, suspension, steel body and fenders to create markets for those vehicles both with middle and working class consumers and with his workers whom he paid generously by contemporary standards. Ford added a metal roof in the mid-twenties. By that time, for all Ford's market power and many loyal buyers, he had saturated the motorized, updated, horse drawn buggy market. When General Motors differentiated vehicle offerings, notably with safer, steel roofs, Ford's market share collapsed.

Alphabet, Amazon, Apple, Facebook, Microsoft and Netflix power a first commercial Internet generation relevance engine originating in main frame search functions analogous to motorizing a horse drawn buggy over distributed networks for advertising revenues.

Each enterprise was the first to dominate its respective market.

All differentiate distinct product competencies: Alphabet/Google with search and content, Amazon with on-line shopping and web services, Apple with music and on-line payments, Facebook with social networks and messaging, Microsoft with office productivity tools and cloud computing, Netflix with mass entertainment distribution on demand. On the surface, these may appear analogous to General Motors brands. In the end, each is, and all are extraction and rendering machines to greater or less extents executing relevance.

Their advertising markets are necessarily in flux. For instance, Google is forecast to lose "digital ad market share"[109] principally due to depressed demand for travel while Amazon's is anticipated to increase due to demand for other goods and services.

One or more could "go the way of the Tin Lizzie"[110] when relevance encounters competition. For instance, *The Verge's* Casey Newton remarked to *The Columbia Journalism Review*[111] in March, 2020: "[I]f you want to challenge Zuckerberg, you just have to come up with a twist on existing communication tools and get a bunch of teenagers to download it."

Artwork by Vito Mattaliano © Hugh Carter Donahue

Facebook's[112] growth in market share in the first quarter of 2019 captured a 25% increase in revenues and 50% decrease in profits from the same quarter in 2018. The firm earned more revenues but greater increases in operating and other costs resulted in less profit. This suggests that the advertising paradigm lives with fresh costs straining profitably. Given an attractive alternative, the marketplace may be ready to morph to a Model A, say shopping and global finance.

Larry Page (Alphabet/Google), Jeff Bezos (Amazon), the late Steve Jobs (Apple), Mark Zuckerberg (Facebook), Bill Gates (Microsoft) and Reed Hastings (Netflix) standout as industry leaders every bit as consequential to Zuboff's surveillance capitalism as Henry Ford was to mass production in industrial capitalism.

If one elects a metaphor from the built environment, advertising paradigm architecture vindicates and embodies relevance's derivative nature and strengths. Relevance measures an outcome of a search. Its architecture extracts and organizes search outcomes for advertising patrons. To be sure, the architecture affords originality, too. Facebook displays individual, enterprise and institution content. Apple features music. Netflix produces entertainment. Amazon publishes. It is all concentric by enticing attention back into advertising paradigm structures for consumption and subscription.

Alphabet, Amazon, Apple, Facebook, Microsoft and Netflix are like Venice with its massive, highly articulated, masonry and limestone, reflective structures serenely floating on Istrian limestone platforms atop water resistant alder pilings driven into Adriatic Sea estuarian mud:

Alphabet/Google: loggia for viewing or searching

Artwork by Vito Mattaliano © Hugh Carter Donahue

Source: Wikipedia, Campbell Library, Rowan University

Amazon: tracery and quatrefoils aggregating specific collections of depictions

Apple, Facebook and Netflix: stained glass depicting social media and entertainment content

Artwork by Vito Mattaliano © Hugh Carter Donahue

Source: Wikipedia, Campbell Library, Rowan University

Microsoft: Ducal Palace and Arsenal exerting operating system command and control

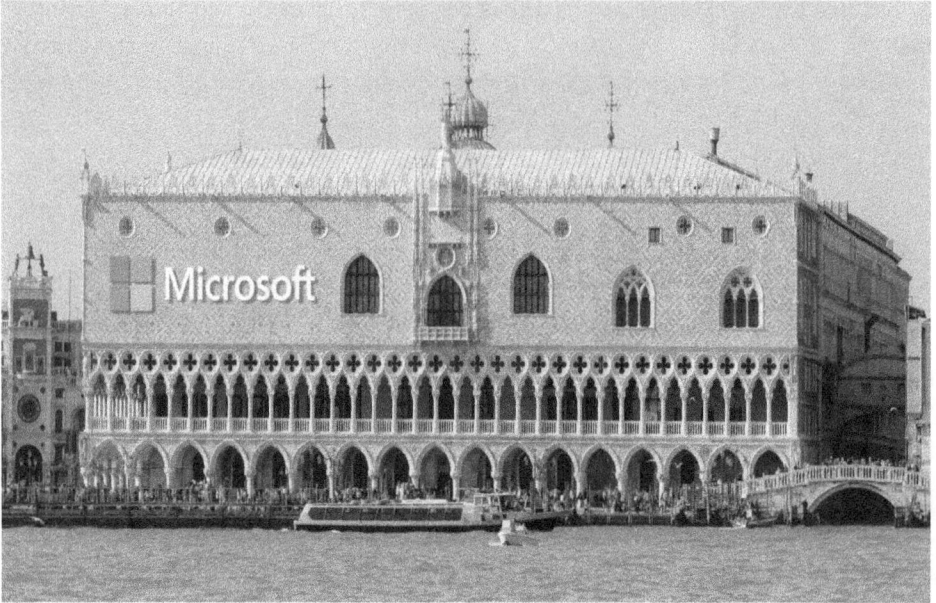

Artwork by Vito Mattaliano © Hugh Carter Donahue

Source: Wikipedia Creative Commons

Microsoft operating systems are custodial managing data, meta data and networks.

Byzantine	Gothic	Renaissance
MS-DOS IBM PC	Windows Office	Azure

"The Ducal Palace, which was the great work of Venice, was built successively in three stages," John Ruskin relays in *Stones of Venice* (1907, Volume II, p. 264, 276). "There was the Byzantine Ducal Palace, a Gothic Ducal Palace, and a Renaissance Ducal Palace. The second superseded the first totally, a few stones of which (if indeed so much) are all that is left. But the third superseded the second in part only and the existing building is formed by the union of the two. There were in it the palace, the state prisons, the senate-house, and the offices of public business; in other words, it was Buckingham Palace, the Tower of olden days, the Houses of Parliament, and Downing Street, all in one; and any of these four portions may be spoken of, without involving an allusion to any other."

Microsoft's Gothic and Renaissance embodiments consolidate the legitimate greatness of the enterprise. Office launched in November, 1985, just about two years after American Telephone & Telegraph divestiture in January, 1984. Office created entrepreneurial opportunities for computer programmers and software engineers adjusting to regional bell operating company creation and management. Office made it possible for these technologists to leave phone companies behind and for recent computer science graduates to seek entrepreneurial wealth creating Office applications. Even if the software sucked[113], trial and error was par for the course in emerging applications markets. Through the last decades of the twentieth century and into the 21st century, the goal emerged to emulate Gates. If one could corner an application for a sector – say energy, or finance or health – he or she could then exert first mover advantage for comparable market power within those sectors.

Such open participation recalls craftsmen constructing Gothic cathedrals from lowliest laborers to gifted glass, stone, tile, terrazzo and masonry artisan each contributing his finest work. This approach animated Microsoft as a catholic-with-a-lower-case "c" enterprise, expressed Bill Gates's commercial and operational genius, and distinguished Microsoft from elegant Apple, which exacted absolute uniformity.

With Azure, announced in 2008 and launched in 2010, Microsoft is unambiguously flourishing in a revenue Renaissance. Azure extends firm capabilities and protracts adopters' dependencies for analytics, storage and productivity across economic sectors. Azure's immediate and long-term capabilities mirror double-entry bookkeeping, which emerged in Europe during the Renaissance. Double-entry bookkeeping, an innovative ledger technology, allowed adopters to ascertain cash flow, profit and loss and receivables and expenditures. At any given moment, a Renaissance enterprise with double-entry ledgers could see whether it was making or losing money. The transparency served as the basis for rational calculation of risk in commerce, shipping and manufacturing. As commerce expanded with consequent requirements for navies to protect ocean trade and armies to safeguard overland shipping, the nation state superseded the city state as modernity emerged in the 16th century. Metaphorically, Azure may well be as consequential for 21st century commerce.

Success, particularly for Microsoft and Amazon, could exert inertia. Amazon reported $60B and its Web Services unit reported just under $8B in first quarter 2019 earnings. Microsoft laid claim to be a trillion-dollar company in 2019 with productivity, cloud and personal computing lines of business each earning approximately $10B in the first quarter of the year. With Windows 10[114] in 2015 and Windows as a service and firmware as a service[115] in 2018, Microsoft is carrying the Ruskin analogy forward. With Azure, Office and Windows, Microsoft is extending operating system command and control[116] as successor platforms to MS-DOS. Nonetheless, each firm would flourish more if it were to adopt intent as a network element.

Jeff Bezos and William Gates command respect as latter day Doge and Admiral Sebastiano Venier of the Republic of Venice, hero of the Battle of Lepanto (1571) consolidating European naval power over the Ottoman Empire.[117]

Artwork by Vito Mattaliano © Hugh Carter Donahue

Sebastiano Venier portrait: By Jacopo Tintoretto - Kunsthistorisches Museum Wien, Bilddatenbank.

Source: Wikipedia, Campbell Library, Rowan University

Advertising paradigm architecture is as much baroque and rococo as Gothic and Renaissance. Internet search and social media, coupled with broadband wireline and wireless networks, afford large spaces for looking up whatever one wants and communicating with whomever one wishes replacing a dome orienting heavenward connecting worshippers with God. All the data and meta data created through search and animated with communications appear like paintings and statues of angels, saints and martyrs commanding attention. Twitter is both gigantic in its mass and import yet light and luminous in individual experiences like Saint Peter's Basilica. Each brand is its own cartouche. Like baroque trompe-l'oiel paintings, slights of deception often appear real. Psychological-political manipulation, a social media nadir during the 2016 presidential election, stimulated illusions with forced perspectives. As social media and entertainment seek scope economies, streaming video, crowd-sourced suggestions for thematic content, on-demand programming, activations for likely purchasers and programs like Amazon's "Transparent" and Netflix's "Orange Is the New Black" humanizing characters depicting wider varieties of gender identities and racial and ethnic backgrounds are essentially rococo offering novelty and theatricality to immerse attention. 'Non-,' 'pan,' 'trans,' 'cis,' and 'poly' prefixes complement norms like 'gender fluidity' and 'sexual fluidity' embodying character attributes in entertainment narratives.

Having it both ways is contradictory, one could rejoin. Alphabet, Amazon, Apple, Facebook, Microsoft and Netflix cannot be vehicles and structures simultaneously. However, both analogies illuminate. Dominant incumbents embody hegemony and dominance analogous to the Doge's Palace or Palazzo Santa Sofia or Ca' Foscari. Venice flourished in part due to its monopoly over glass making technologies in addition to its naval strength. Analogously, Alphabet, Amazon, Apple, Facebook, Microsoft and Netflix afford ways of seeing by commanding and controlling Internet commerce using the advertising paradigm through relevance extracted from fluctuating individual, enterprise and institutional searches. Aside from regulatory fines imposed on Facebook and Google, none of the incumbents has suffered any fundamental setback to its lines of business analogous to the Serene Republic's evaporating dominance[118] over spice trading, textile manufacturing and book publishing from early in the 17th century to Napoleon's invasion in 1796.

Regulatory corrections, while often initially promising, only go so far. For instance, if the European Union actually enforces General Data Protection Regulation rigorously, this could be tantamount to a contemporaneous Code Napoleon[119] curtailing dominant advertising incumbent market power. As Dr. Johnny Ryan[120], Ph.D., Brave Chief Policy and Industry Relations Officer, pointed out in Senate Judiciary Committee testimony in May, 2019, "today, big tech companies create cascading monopolies by leveraging users' data from one line of business to dominate other lines of business too. This hurts nascent competitors, stifles innovation and reduces consumer choice. However, two elements in the GDPR can fix this – if they are enforced. First, Article 5(1)(b), is the "purpose limitation" principle, which ring fences personal data held by companies so they can't use it outside of consumer expectations. They need a legal basis for each data processing purpose. Second, Article 7 (3) requires that an opt-in must be as easy to undo as it was to give in the first place, and that people can do so without detriment…. [T]hings are looking bleak for our colleagues at Google and Facebook. Their year-over-year growth declined steadily in Europe since the GDPR – despite a buoyant advertising market. They face multiple investigations and it is very likely that they will be forced to change how they do business."[121]

Unfortunately, Ryan reported that EU member states are not funding data protection authorities adequately to enforce regulation. In a thoughtful, April, 2020 analysis, Ryan recommended that "national governments…invest in far more specialist tech investigators, pay competitive salaries to attract top talent, and … provide the finance to allow data protection authorities to pursue adversarial enforcement." The European Union would wisely "establish a tech investigative unit to support national data protection authorities" and "launch an infringement procedure against EU countries that fail to implement Article 52(4) of the GDPR,"[122] he advises.

Stanford economists notice the limits of extending the advertising paradigm to cloud computing, artificial intelligence and machine learning. Dominant Internet monopolists and oligopolists' main challenge is pretending that the 'free data' Internet affords leisure when it is work. That initial, commercial Internet conceit of convincing individuals, enterprises and institutions that all are cultivating "dignity" pursuing "leisure" is the central problem, they see[123]. Sticking to this conceit misdirects research and development investment in cloud computing, machine learning, artificial intelligence and the Internet of Things by focusing too much on relevance for advertising placement.

Artificial intelligence research and development fuels targeted advertising rather than productivity, the economists[124] observe. Virtually all initial artificial intelligence systems relied on hard coding, they note, impairing scaling. With no incentive to individuals, enterprise or institutions to enhance the quantity or quality of data due to advertising paradigm extraction and rendition, AI scaling is all the more elusive.

Machine learning research and development focuses on automation to perfect relevance. In machine learning, optimal representation for reinforcement[125] analyzes non-linear mapping for finer predictive analytics, specifically "value functions… shaping…agent representation," to "open up the possibility of automatically generating auxiliary tasks in deep reinforcement learning, analogous to how deep learning itself enabled a move away from hand-crafted features."[126] This emphasis begins a foundation for automatically computing predictive analytics and to that extent it contributes to scaling machine learning. If the approach yields, it would scale enabling technologies for extensible advertising paradigm extraction and rendition within the reinforcement learning approach to machine learning, for supervised and unsupervised machine learning research may yield greater efficiencies.

All the focus on relevance for advertising, however, deflects from research and development enhancing productivity where machine learning could and would likely achieve transformative yields. Until intent is factored in, opportunities to develop and apply machine learning to enhance productivity will likely remain fallow.

In virtual reality, speed's the thing. Advanced sensory and measurement systems support dynamic methods for analyzing data extraction and metadata rendition through real time capture of sensory and measurement data in immersive environments. "Our guiding observation," Alexey Dosovitskiy and Vladlen Koltun observe, "is that the interlocked temporal structure of the sensory and measurement streams provides a rich supervisory signal… [T]he agent can be trained to predict the effect of different actions on future measurements. Assuming that the goal can be expressed in terms of future measurements, predicting these provides all the information necessary to support action. This reduces sensorimotor control to supervised learning, while supporting learning from raw experience and without extraneous data. Supervision is provided by experience itself: by acting and observing the effects of different actions in the context of changing sensory inputs and goals."[127] Certainly, fast ("one step of the agent is equivalent to 114 milliseconds of real time")[128] in immersive video game environments.

Regarding cloud services, seamlessly connected private infrastructure across multiple providers defines innovation. A knowledgeable observer reports that Amazon Web Services, Microsoft Azure and Google Cloud Platform have the largest market shares for infrastructure as a service yet innovations in artificial intelligence and machine learning open each's platform to competition. Just under $4T is in play in global IT markets with software as a service as a growing sector. Opacities hamper adoptions. "…Oracle used to break out infrastructure-, platform- and software-as-a-service in its financial reports. Today, Oracle's cloud business is lumped together. Microsoft has a 'commercial cloud' that is very successful, but also hard to parse. IBM has cloud revenue and 'as-a-service' revenue. Google doesn't break out cloud revenue at all. Aside from AWS, parsing cloud sales has become more difficult," he observes. Amazon

Web Services is pitching artificial intelligence and machine learning to place itself as "a key cog" in adopter cloud data base markets, for enterprise customers loom large in AWS's orbit as it strives to become "entrenched for decades to come as it continues to evolve services and sell them." Microsoft Azure, number two in market size to Amazon Web Services with estimated $11B annual revenues offers 'cloud-meets-data center' functionalities across infrastructure, platforms and applications. Notably, Microsoft is cultivating artificial intelligence to provide its adopters to "reason over" consolidated data, and this could be a powerful inertial current toward recurrent revenues with increased dependencies over years of use. Google Cloud Platform with $4B annual revenues is offering price competition with AWS and Microsoft to win customers. IBM with $12.2B in annual cloud revenues is reaching out to customers following its $34B Red Hat merger and acquisition for "hybrid open" cloud functionalities and consolidated management across platforms, analysis, quantum computing and Watson. IBM promises "secure portability of data and workloads across cloud environments,… consistency in management and security protocols" across clouds together with flexibility to mitigate being locked into a single provider. Cisco, Oracle, SAP, Salesforce, Workday have distinct strengths.[129]

Cloud network elements are in play as novel data and metadata for monetization and commercialization. They afford insight into intent, but have yet to trigger it amid profoundly inertial currents inuring to relevance.

For all the abundant promise, research and development do not afford adequate confidence clarifying the integrity and authenticity of 5G, artificial intelligence, machine learning, and the Internet of Things at this point in time. None of those technologies can scale nor can the cloud computing on which they would run and rely without incentives and reciprocities rewarding intent.

Other challenges beset relevance and the advertising paradigm. After consolidating market dominance and advancing consumer welfare[130] from the mid to late nineties into the unit decade of the 21st century, the advertising paradigm's enabling strength of measuring relevance is now provoking disturbing issues of trust and abuses of market power. This, in turn, suggests it is time to move beyond Internet practices of trading privacy for efficiency and mobility. Legislative and regulatory remedies encompass breaking up[131] dominant, incumbent enterprises, notably Facebook, into separate companies, fines, remote data[132] collection clarifications and restrictions, and inquiries addressing consent agreement compliance and industry standards and practices in varying degrees, one way or another, addressing market power and competition.[133]

For instance, innovation slows down. "A result of diminished competition is that the pace of innovation slows," The Verge's Casey Newton remarked to The Columbia Journalism Review, in March, 2020. "We have to wait longer for the next Evan Spiegel to emerge and give us ephemeral messaging and stories. Or for the next TikTok to come along and give us duets and a feed that works even before you follow anyone."[134]

Mark Zuckerberg's call for regulation in March, 2019 elicited appraisals and estimations regarding regulatory inoculation for relevance and the advertising paradigm. Perhaps Facebook wishes to emulate AT&T as a regulated monopoly in its newsfeed line of business following the example of Theodore Vail's and Nathan Kingsbury's commitment to universal service in 1913. Facebook may wish to repurpose unfeasible broadcast and cable industry regulatory regimes for news and politics to safeguard advertising revenue. A gimlet eyed observer may well chuck up Zuckerberg's call[135] for new Internet rules and regulations as so much public policy click bait[136]. What better way to sustain ingenuity and inventiveness than to focus legislative attention and regulatory scrutiny on established concerns? "Whenever a reliable indicator becomes a target (of social, economic or organizational policy) it ceases to be a reliable indicator," economist Charles Goodhart memorably observed as risk analyst David M. Rowe[137] points out in a thoughtful commentary on risk adaptation.

Facebook founder Chris Hughes contends that Mark Zuckerberg is proposing too little too late. Hughes is calling for structural separation of Instagram and WhatsApp on grounds of monopoly power suppressing innovation and competition to the detriment of the public interest. "Facebook's business model is built on capturing as much of our attention as possible to encourage people to create and share more information about who they are and who they want to be. We pay for Facebook with our data and our attention, and by either measure it doesn't come cheap,"[138] he observes in a May, 2019 commentary.

Brendan Blumer, Block.one CEO, is exact regarding the Block.one capabilities addressing advertising paradigm shortcomings. "Outdated technology and outdated business models" skew rewards to "an elite few"[139] reaping the wealth of individual, enterprise and institution attention, content and data. Block.one employs digital currencies to authenticate and animate participation.

Brave[140] offers a browser that affords privacy and offers a coin-based system for individuals to patronize publishers to address advertising paradigm disintermediation. In June, 2020, Brave apologized for opacity regarding affiliate linking.[141]

These significant, defined participation vehicles, both employing digital currencies, portend rewarding intent.

For instance, in June, 2019, with admirable forethought articulated across Libra documents, Facebook launched Libra[142] with a number of other enterprises and members[143] as a not for profit organization overseeing a crypto-currency for global shopping, payments and banking. Initially named Calibra, the crypto-currency will enable mobile payments inside a digital wallet called Novi, perhaps seeding a fresh walled garden. Patrons can readily link to Facebook and WhatsAPP should they wish. In a series of white papers, the Libra Association addressed governance[144], funding and reserve assets[145], initial technical specifications[146] and membership. "We believe that collaborating and innovating with the financial sector, including regulators and experts across a variety of industries, is the only way to ensure that a sustainable, secure, and trusted framework underpins this new system," it stated. Mark Zuckerberg's testimony before Senate and House banking and financial services committees in July expressed this orientation. Unambiguously, following news feed and social media scandals in the 2016 presidential election, Facebook keenly grasped advertising paradigm attenuations, vulnerabilities and increasingly costly failures if it were to persist with conduct in any way comparable to its earlier episodes with Cambridge Analytica, candidate organizations and abuses of its WhatsApp line of business.

In March, 2020, Alex Kantrowitz, author of *Always Day One How The Tech Titans Plan to Stay On Top Forever*[147] and The Verge journalist Casey Newton shared their ideas about competition and structural separation with Columbia Journalism Review's Mathew Ingram[148]: 'In my book, I argue that we should seriously consider splitting some of these companies apart,' says Kantrowitz. 'Smaller entities would need to compete for suppliers by setting better terms: In Amazon's case that's the small businesses that sell things through its website. In Facebook and Google's case that's media companies producing the content that fill their feeds.' Newton says he is 'generally positive about the idea of Facebook being forced to spin off WhatsApp and Instagram,'[149] although separating them may be more complicated than it seems."

"I believe that Facebook, Google, and Amazon should be seen as out-and-out monopolists that have harmed the American economy in various ways, and have the potential to do much greater harm should their implicit power go uncurbed," Dipayan Ghosh, Kennedy School of Government at Harvard University, argued in Terms of Disservice: How Silicone Valley is Destructive By Design[150], in June, 2020.

Few episodes illustrate the fragility of relevance and the advertising paradigm more vividly than the plights of Twitter and Facebook. Twitter abandoned interactive computer service provider limited liability shield protections created in enabling legislation. After a week or more of urban unrest and mass demonstrations, Facebook edged away from its classically liberal posture in the marketplace of ideas that individuals, enterprises and institutions retain rights to decide the veracity and dubiety they attach to one or another information content provider publication and suppressed video in a Trump campaign tweet pending clarification of copyright. Instead, Facebook employed copyright infringement[151] as it sought some way forward balancing impartiality obligations with its policies concerning veracity and fake news.

For each enterprise, decision making typified firm sensitivity to individuals, enterprises and institutions patronizing its services and, as consequentially, addressing the toxicity many staff attached to President Trump's posts and tweets. The former attested to systemic advertising paradigm infirmities. Would individuals, enterprises and institutions bolt and with them the gravy trains of data and meta data generating voluminous advertising revenues, indispensable to each's business models? Would staff sensitivities confound production? The latter expressed enterprise dependence on their workers and embodied a movement moment.

As Frances Fox Piven remarked earlier in the year during the coronavirus pandemic, "I think that the great untapped reservoir of power—leverage—that ordinary people have is always their ability to refuse to cooperate. Because society is a system of cooperation. That's what economies are, too. And this kind of power, or influence, is not usually exercised. People go along. They like normal life. They prefer normal life to the anxiety provoked by what is abnormal or disorderly. But this is such a period of change and crisis, where the future of American society—of the planet—is at stake. I think it's a time that people would be ready to act on this tacit power that they have to simply refuse to play their normal role in economic relations, in family relations, in community relations, and in political relations. And that happens from time to time. That's when we get our movement moments," she observed in a Mother Jones interview[152].

In June, 2020, noncooperation[153] by enough workers and executives within Twitter and Facebook evidently animated Twitter's initial and Facebook's subsequent abandonment of Section 230 standards with the attendant limited liability shield protections.

Mark Zuckerberg's acknowledgement indicated as much. "We're going to review potential options for handling violating or partially-violating content aside from the binary leave-it-up or take-it-down decisions," he conveyed to Facebook associates in early June. "I know many of you think we should have labeled the President's posts in some way last week. Our current policy is that if content is actually inciting violence, then the right mitigation is to take that content down -- not let people continue seeing it behind a flag. There is no exception to this policy for politicians or newsworthiness. I think this policy is principled and reasonable, but I also respect a lot of the people who think there may be better alternatives, so I want to make sure we hear all those ideas…. In general, I worry that this approach has a risk of leading us to editorialize on content we don't like even if it doesn't violate our policies, so I think we need to proceed very carefully."[154]

The poignancy of Mark Zuckerberg's decision-making evoked Emerson[155]. Its outcome, a policy that Facebook would designate information content provider posts as 'newsworthy'[156] when staff deemed the content violated policy and would not suppress sharing, seemed like a good faith effort at pragmatic resolution. Facebook announced the policy in late June, 2020 during a widespread boycott. Staff passions to suppress political speech unambiguously trammeled and trampled Facebook's congressionally authorized Section 230 discretion as an interactive computer service and exposed the firm to regulatory sanctions and legal action. In August, 2020, Facebook suppressed[157] one of President Trump's posts on the grounds that it conveyed erroneous Covid-19 information.

Facebook policy banning political advertising the week prior to the 2020 presidential election is a similar piece. "We're going to block new political and issue ads during the final week of the campaign…We're…limiting forwarding on Messenger. You'll still be able to share information about the election, but we'll limit the number of chats you can forward a message to at one time,"[158] Mark Zuckerberg announced in early September.

Similarly, Google restricted The Federalist from generating advertising revenue[159] on the grounds that an article in its comments section promoted violence by reporting that some media did not adequately cover looting and violence in connection with Floyd protests. Then, Google[160] issued a statement that it had not demonetized The Federalist but had simply threatened to do so if more, similar content was forthcoming. Senator Ted Cruz (R-Texas) jumped in. "Google is abusing its monopoly power to silence competitors. Google today has become like the empire in Star Wars and what they're doing with this step is testing the death star. They need to stop this right now,"[161] he remarked in a Fox News interview. This occurred after suspending Zero Hedge for several months on the basis of erroneous information, news reports indicated[162]. These are, inescapably, advertising monetizing decisions based on a publication's content whether that content is in a comment section or published by the content provider, the cornerstone of editing as a publisher.

As to the nuts and bolts of what's transpiring. Beyond instructing the Federal Trade Commission and Federal Communications Commission to freshly examine social media platforms' limited liability shields, President Trump directed the Department of Justice to work with state attorneys general to examine applicable state law addressing, "(i) increased scrutiny of users based on the other users they choose to follow, or their interactions with other users; (ii) algorithms to suppress content or users based on indications of political alignment or viewpoint; (iii) differential policies allowing for otherwise impermissible behavior, when committed by accounts associated with the Chinese Communist Party or other anti-democratic associations or governments; (iv) reliance on third-party entities, including contractors, media organizations, and individuals, with indicia of bias to review content; and (v) acts that limit the ability of users with particular viewpoints to earn money on the platform compared with other users similarly situated."[163]

Google accommodations with the People's Republic of China also inflected presidential action: "One United States company, for example, created a search engine for the Chinese Communist Party that would have blacklisted searches for 'human rights,' hid data unfavorable to the Chinese Communist Party, and tracked users determined appropriate for surveillance. It also established research partnerships in China that provide direct benefits to the Chinese military," the executive order notes.

Through these and other actions, search and social media giants merited fresh regulatory scrutiny for moving well beyond limited liability shield protections. "Section 230 was not intended to allow a handful of companies to grow into titans controlling vital avenues for our national discourse under the guise of promoting open forums for debate, and then to provide those behemoths blanket immunity when they use their power to censor content and silence viewpoints that they dislike. When an interactive computer service provider removes or restricts access to content and its actions do not meet the criteria…, it is engaged in editorial conduct. It is the policy of the United States that such a provider should properly lose the limited liability shield… and be exposed to liability like any traditional editor and publisher that is not an online provider,"[164] President Trump indicated in the executive order.

It is not simply an American challenge. In April, 2020, as the coronavirus decimated newspaper advertising, the Australian Competition and Consumer Commission[165] announced policies impelling Google and Facebook to compensate publishers for news content.

There are also fresh challenges with marketers and advertisers. Cookies are fading out and intent is up for grabs. For instance, "you can buy an "intender" audience from just about any publisher or third-party data aggregator," Scott Kelliher, head of US brand advertising and partnerships for eBay Advertising, remarked to Smart Brief in May, 2020. "The catch is, the data they use to define intent isn't typically based on true intent signals. Mostly, it's contextually-based or broadly defined behaviors that won't necessarily perform... And…third-party data providers don't provide the transparency or robust set of intent signals that advertisers need to power successful campaigns."[166]

In these ways, internal vulnerabilities and negative externalities barnacle relevance and encumber the advertising paradigm and the commercial Internet to delay, hold back, impede the course of, or retard scaling Internet and broadband mass production. On June 25, 2020, within a month of the President's executive order and two months of the Australian initiative, Google indicated that it will begin compensating more publishers for news. "This program will help participating publishers monetize their content…," a news release reported. "…[A]n enhanced storytelling experience that lets people go deeper into more complex stories" extended relevance and the advertising paradigm as does an "offer to pay for free access for users to read paywalled articles on a publisher's site. This will let paywalled publishers grow their audiences and open an opportunity for people to read content they might not ordinarily see," according to the statement.[167] So doing also extended the Google News Initiative[168] and built on an emergency funding program.[169]

Hence, concerns arose that in compensating some news organizations, Google would leverage its monopoly power in search to bias information available to the public by demurring on compensating news organizations publishing content at odds with staff sensitivities. While ostensibly immensely healthy for publishers, the initiative alarmed of a tightening Gordian Knot scaling Google dominion over search, journalism and consciousness. Earlier accommodations with the Chinese Communist Party made for pause.

Chapter Three details Known Paradigm efficiencies and efficacies addressing and overcoming these advertising paradigm shortcomings with available technologies.

KNOWN
Paradigm
Efficiencies
&
Efficacies

CHAPTER THREE

Known Paradigm Efficiencies & Efficacies

Known Paradigm efficiencies and efficacies power egalitarian wealth creation at no marginal cost by activating intent and reciprocity as network elements.

Voluminous, distinct, various, discrete and recurrent transactions scale Internet and broadband mass production buying and selling data and meta data.

New markets clearing finance and communications as well as 21st century credit worthiness, artificial intelligence, climate and bio-technology risks become increasingly reciprocal and transparent.

The Known Paradigm affords symmetrical transparency to illuminate and score risk. Individual, enterprise and institution can authenticate monetary and risk values of data and meta data any and all wish to transact and to be known. With these capabilities, any and all can reach decisions to trust whether or not to participate in transactions. Each and all can generate wealth with paradigm functionalities to address shifting risks.[170]

A multi-point to multi-point polyhedron[171] depicts paradigm geometry. All participants hold and grant rights. Each embodies and all bestow dignity.

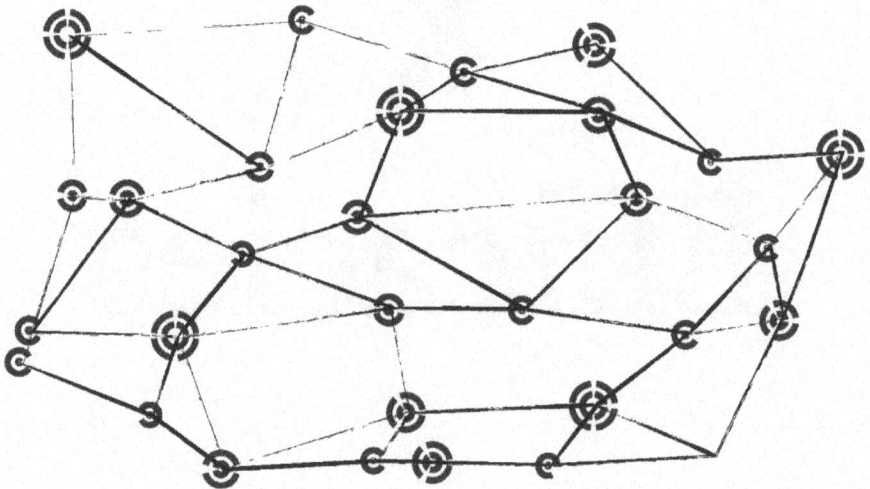

Artwork by Vito Mattaliano © Hugh Carter Donahue

The paradigm's polyhedron geometry self-sustains through the diversity and individuality of individuals, enterprises and institutions dynamically creating and transacting digital wealth for and among themselves in multi-point-to-multi-point, transparent, permissioned transactions.

Known Paradigm polyhedron geometry may, in fact, power its most consequential contribution of enhancing consciousness by spurring individual, enterprise and institution imaginations (e.g., "imagination is more important than knowledge. For knowledge is limited, whereas imagination encircles the world,"[172] Albert Einstein observed).

By originating intent as a fresh network element, the Known Paradigm powers imagination. Individuals, enterprises and institutions can express each's distinct consciousness. By so doing they create more and more choices. The choices generate increasing value through reciprocal, transparent, mass-produced data and meta data transactions. The paradigm's great, countervailing, restorative, liberating capaciousness is the exact opposite of advertising paradigm micro manipulation of "intimate emotional-based data" in Frederick Lowen's insightful turn of phrase.

The Known Paradigm equips technologists, investors and adopters with standards to develop and measure the integrity and authenticity of all this data and meta data mass production. Repeatable trial and error monetizing and measuring the real and near real time values of individual-enterprise-and-institution-permissioned data and meta data through origination, deployment and disposition becomes feasible.

Recall Claude Shannon's main frame paradigm classifying and typifying source, transmitter, channel, receiver and destination.

Recall Gordon Moore's foresight regarding doubling of microchip transistors every two years as computer prices halve.

Recall Paul W. Litchfield's appreciation of reciprocity in industrial capitalism.

The Known Paradigm now exerts comparable capabilities to develop and measure network elements powering egalitarian wealth creation.

By rationalizing trust, the paradigm stimulates aggregate demand. With immeasurably more participants buying and selling data and metadata securely, larger markets with more diverse participants complement those for advertising relevance. Data and metadata recurrently increase in value with each individual, enterprise or institution transaction through the life cycle of any transaction and its underlying assets as well as on its own as new, verifiable, information-rich network elements.

By stimulating aggregate demand, the paradigm contributes to resolving persistent wealth and income inequality.[173] With greater numbers of individuals, enterprises and institutions transacting data and metadata with bitcoins over block chains, business volumes and asset values increase in virtuous cycles.

New markets would encourage investment and employment and would create wealth. Recent tax policy exerted salutary effects on dividends and stock buy-backs but have been less effective stimulating investment.

Relevance and the advertising paradigm can get deserved rest. The pernicious trade-off of surrendering privacy for communication efficiency becomes inefficient; that is, too costly chasing stochastic consumption acts and narrowly defined monitoring factors (e.g., ambient temperature) or conditions (health indicators). Individual, enterprise and institution data and meta data control and autonomy become the norms.

Taylorism, scientific management and 20th century industrial capitalism rewarded and reciprocated worker initiative with incentives to improve efficiency and increase productivity enriching worker, manager and enterprise. In the late 20th and early 21st centuries, relevance and the advertising paradigm decimated reciprocity. In the process, the commercial Internet spawned wealth disparities recalling[174] those of the Gilded Age[175].

Dominant Internet search and social media incumbents like Google, Facebook and Twitter could deploy Known Paradigm capabilities to establish 21st century standards of care now that regulators and state attorney generals are scrutinizing Section 230 standards and practices that enabled relevance and the advertising paradigm. Known Paradigm living contracts™ and immutable records enable burden shifting to information content providers. All the transaction and reputational injury costs that Google, Facebook and Twitter inflict on themselves with arbitrary and capricious censoring could and would no longer afflict the firms. The paradigm's vastly more robust elements go well beyond crafting exculpatory or hold-harmless legal language. All the relevant standards and practices in contract and defamation law would remain undisturbed. Attorneys could and would cultivate trial and error prosecuting and defending claims of torts of defamation. Like anything new, as relevance and the advertising paradigm once were, it is unknowable whether and how libel and defamation law may evolve. For instance, litigation between an information service provider and an aggrieved party may trigger fresh evaluation of New York Times v. Sullivan libel standards. Certainly, there're plenty of statutes and constitutional decisions for guidance and definition. The critical value-adds of large incumbent adoption of Known Paradigm capabilities are the reductions of uncertainty concerning Section 230 and creating business models to thrive as cookies fade out and relevance receives well-earned rest.

Many innovations are feasible. Novi could come alive for Facebook and other Libra Association members with Known Paradigm digital currency innovations. Microsoft Office 365 Money in Excel[176] would thrive, too. Money In Excel aggregates, integrates, monitors, displays and summarizes transactions. Credit card, bank account, loan and investment transactions automatically link to and display in Excel spreadsheets. KNOWN digital currencies, living contracts™ and immutable records support intent for readier individual, enterprise and institution adoption. With these functionalities, the digital wallet and the subscription feature could easily complement Azure and other productivity features for Micorsoft's Renaissance cathedral superseding Office, Redmond's Gothic basilica. With increased volumes and enhanced asset values, dominant incumbents will be better able to withstand and to thrive in democratic markets.

The same is as true for reshoring supply chains and revitalizing American manufacturing. Incumbent supply chains are legacy systems animated by Secretary of State Henry Kissinger's 1971 visit to China and dating from China's 2001 membership in the World Trade Organization. While the coronavirus may have shattered some and shaken virtually all, supply chains, particularly those relying on investment in domestic manufacturing, will require goodly amounts of time, effort and vision to be created and maintained. In that regard, Known Paradigm transparencies expedite reshoring. Much of the commentary calls for public investment or federal government mandates. The Known Paradigm both complements and obsolesces such approaches at the same time it makes it possible for the parties creating supply chains to pay themselves for the data and meta data they create doing the work. Logistics, of course, are the crowning glory of paradigm capabilities, for one can more ably control assets and investment thanks to paradigm transparencies.

For the poor, paradigm capabilities create pathways to income and wealth buying and selling data and meta data. As with supply chains, these challenges are a long time in the making, longer concerning historic discrimination. Among its many virtues, the Known Paradigm enables narrowly tailored implementation directing wealth creation. At the same time the paradigm is agnostic to race, national origin and the rest. In these ways, the Known Paradigm could and would create self-selecting, self-empowering platforms validating participants for their distinct ingenuities requiring no public investment with its own partisan contentions and taxpayer burden.

Innovations and efficacies obsolesce antagonisms between individual and employer. It is noteworthy that John Ruskin pointed out the strengths and weaknesses of scientific management prior to Taylor's publication of his consequential contribution to industrial capitalism. "You must either make a tool of the creature, or a man of him. You cannot make both," Ruskin points out in The Stones of Venice, (1907, II, p.147 ff) "Men are not intended to work with the accuracy of tools, to be precise and perfect in all their actions. If you will have that precision out of them, and make their fingers measure degrees like cog-wheels, and their arms strike curves like compasses, you must unhumanise them. All the energy of their spirits must be given to make cogs and compasses of themselves. All their attention and strength must go to the accomplishment of the mean act… that it may not err from its steely precision, and so soul and sight be worn away, and the whole human being be lost at last…., saved only by its Heart, which cannot go into the form of cogs and compasses, but expands, after ten hours are over, into fireside humanity…. It is not that men are ill fed, but that they have no pleasure in the work by which they make their bread and therefore look to wealth as the only means to pleasure…. On the other hand, if you will make a man of the working creature, you cannot make a tool. Let him but begin to imagine, to think, to do anything worth doing; and the engine-tuned precision is lost at once. Out come all his roughness, all his dullness, all his incapability…but out comes the whole majesty of him…there will be transfiguration." Paradigm capabilities address all variances – exceptional as well as dull, fine as well as crude, for individual, enterprise and institution wealth creation.

And, for the indifferent, the paradigm incents Internet adoption by rewarding use. "Consistently, the U.S. Census Bureau surveys reveal that the primary cause for non-adoption is a lack of interest in what the Internet offers," economist George S. Ford[177] notes in a thoughtful, July 2020 study.

Innovations advance responsive web design. Separately, Ethan Marcotte observes that "responsive web design offers us a way forward,… allowing us to 'design for the ebb and flow of things…' Now more than ever, we're designing work meant to be viewed along a gradient of different experiences.' "[178] The paradigm inflects such dynamism.

Paradigm scope and scale qualitatively and quantitatively supersede advertising paradigm precise, multi-point-to-point consumption inducement. By reifying search as relevance, the advertising paradigm goes no further than advertising placement. Stilling functionalities at alluring consumption arrests transition to anything livelier.

Known Paradigm innovations, by contrast, refine data and metadata to mass production. "Analytics readily incorporate fresh with incumbent data for efficient clarity," Ramesh Venkataramaiah, KNOWN Head of Data, remarks. These capabilities are analogous to Charles F. Kettering's with electric starters (1911) and tetraethyllead gasoline for internal combustion engines in motor vehicles (1921) by charging ignition and powering movement "from a past to a new state."

"Innovations are disruptive and/or evolutionary," Bill Hartnett, KNOWN Chief Strategy and Innovation Officer points out.

As disruptive technologies, such capacious strengths unshackle search relevance chaining individuals, enterprises and institution to dominant incumbents impelling them to give over data and give up privacy in return for Internet functionality and efficiency. They also empower new entrants offering substitutes. For instance, advertisers could curtail advertising fraud loses[179], and publishers[180] could gain greater precision reaching readers and consumers.

The advertising paradigm is distinctly costly to publishers by creating spot markets through real time bidding for advertising placements. "Real-time data leakage" allows third party intermediaries to collect data about publishers' audiences and target those audiences cheaper elsewhere. "Real-time revenue leakage" sees 80%-55% of publisher revenue captured by adtech companies… Ad fraud diverts revenue from publishers, and may also undermine advertisers' trust and willingness to spend on digital advertising," reported Johnny Ryan, Brave Chief Policy and Industry Relations Officer[181]. The advertising paradigm virtually imprisons publishers in withering relevance claws, an online publishers[182] trade association attests.

By creating rewarded connections between readers and publishers, paradigm capabilities lower reader costs, boost publisher revenues and enhance speed for each and all in addition to dispensing with advertising clutter.

As evolutionary technologies, innovations pathway dominant incumbent business models for democratic markets to complement advertising revenues and enable each to extend extensive data archives.

For instance, as Facebook cultivates shopping[183] and global finance[184] with its Libra cryptocurrency, Known Paradigm functionalities would swell volumes and create actionable, valuable data and metadata, generate vendor or seller sales and lower buyer purchase and transaction costs securely. This is in addition to their value-adds regarding defamation litigation.

The significance is straightforward. Individuals, enterprises and institutions could set cloud computing standards and practices to specifically tailored functionalities. They could manage costs and determine vendor selection and exit. All could monitor and clarify exactly what it is that one's paying for. All could control privacy and security and address regulatory obligations. Incumbents would find it easier to develop trial and error testing more efficiently as they develop and offer new products and services.

Innovations and efficacies could scale adoption and deployment of 5G wireless and wireline telecommunications, the Internet of Things, bitcoins and block chains. Until intent is incented and rewarded, these technologies confound dominant incumbent research and development investment and marketing strategies.

Through these dynamic capabilities, paradigm functionalities resolve advertising paradigm regulatory costs. Individual, enterprise and institution intent effect consumer welfare by dispatching monopolistic advertising paradigm market power price inflation. Intent is faster, more effective and less costly than drafting legislation or crafting regulation attempting to reform anachronistic anti-trust law relying on consumer pricing as the sole standard for legally permissible mergers and acquisitions. While directing regulators to "look at the full value-chain"[185] determining anti-competitive, advertising paradigm market power abuses is laudable, regulators too often focus on corporate sector employment upon retirement from public service. This virtually irresistible career force constrains effective regulation. Furthermore, time consuming legislative and regulatory processes impel engaging experts and legal counsel. With this expertise, dominant incumbents too often inflect rules and regulations containing costs for prior abuses and leaving them free for new ventures. Industry self-regulation[186] supporting yet another bureaucracy perhaps charged with enforcing voluntary standards becomes unnecessary, too, with real time and near real time monitoring and scoring.

The Known Paradigm resolves challenges managing innovation and supporting competition in international finance. "[T]he issue...is how to promote data-sharing," the Bank of International Settlements noted in its 2019 report. "Currently, data ownership is rarely clearly assigned. For practical purposes, the default outcome is that big techs have de facto ownership of customer data, and customers cannot (easily) grant competitors access to their relevant information. This uneven playing field between customers and service providers can be remedied somewhat by assigning data property rights to the customers. Customers could then decide with which providers to share or sell data. In effect, this attempts to resolve inefficiencies through the allocation of property rights and the creation of a competitive market for data – the decentralised or "Coasian" solution.... However, the mapping between the policy tools and the ultimate outcomes is more complex in the case of big techs. The DNA feedback loop challenges a smooth application of the Coasian approach. The reason is twofold. First, big techs can obtain additional data from their own ecosystems (social networking, search, e-commerce, etc.), outside the financial services they operate. Second, data have increasing returns to scope and scale – a single additional piece of data (e.g., a credit score) has more value when combined with an existing large stock of data – and economies of scope – e.g., when used in the supply of a broader range of services. For both reasons, data have more value to big techs. In a bidding market for data, big techs would most likely outbid their competitors. Letting market forces freely run their course could not be guaranteed to result in the desired (competitive) outcomes. Concretely, if banks' customers were to grant (or sell) big techs unrestricted access to their banking data, this could reinforce the DNA feedback loop and paradoxically increase big techs' competitive advantage over banks, as opposed to keeping it in check."[187]

Paradigm efficacies and efficiencies rationalize transactions to create dynamic equilibria among banks and big tech. Data frames, data incentives, data marketplaces and bit coins powered by top speed distributed ledgers embody secure markets for all varieties of participants beyond banks and big tech. Immutable records memorialize all transactions.

Bitcoins and block chains have yet to scale. As matters now stand, bitcoins and block chains are too labor intense. Simply on their own terms, any arithmetic change to a bitcoin in any block chain animates logarithmic transaction costs. As with any innovation, provenance takes time till risk measurement and scoring are established, and at this point in time uncertainty and opacity[188] retard transparent risk determination. Relevance cannot address these challenges. Relevance cannot illuminate distinct bitcoins traversing discreet block chains over petabytes and zettabytes of data flooding, crowding and congesting bitcoins and block chains. By definition, relevance remains re-active by measuring the outcome of a search, not the initiation of an intent. This is the heart of the matter with bitcoins and block chains. Individuals, enterprises and institutions wish to adopt bitcoins and blockchains as vehicles to monetize intent separate from fiat currencies. By clarifying bitcoin and block chain value, Known innovations yield transparency enabling verifiable risk. Once risk is measured transparently and scored systematically, bitcoins and blockchains can and would scale as either as commodities or as currencies.

Hence, KNOWN Paradigm contributions create and enhance transparency by clarifying regulatory costs and uncertainties going forward with digital commodities and currencies in 21st century economies. Bitcoins, block chains, stable coins, secure tokens can and will increasingly emerge during trial and error of creating and scaling digital currencies as advertising paradigm infirmities obsolesce its reliability and utility. All implicate securities[189] and commodities[190] law and regulation, which are striving to promote innovation while safeguarding investor and consumer welfare. By enabling counterparties to see the risk and monetary values of what a party is offering through digital coin and token platforms, paradigm capabilities immediately detect unlawful offerings. Systemically and systematically, paradigm innovations and efficacies create the basis for reliability and replicability with digital currencies by affording transparencies to address regulatory obligations.

There are other challenges. Bitcoins and block chains continue to be volatile and scandal ridden despite recent adoption by a major bank[191] realizing instantaneous transvaluation from its bitcoin currency to United States dollars. This interbank information network[192] includes more than 200 member banks and is focusing on secure messaging, document file transfer and data modelling for settlements. As for volatility, a ceo's death or reported death[193] in December, 2018 froze $145M cryptocurrency in an offline or cold wallet in January, 2019 and highlighted the importance of sedulous monitoring and control over private keys and bitcoin currencies. Bitcoin volatility limits adoption. Asset values can grow exponentially or crash catastrophically in a heartbeat. The bitcoin "does not have the capabilities right now to become an effective currency," Twitter and Square CEO Jack Dorsey[194] remarked in March, 2018. Fraud[195] is a constant challenge. "Mass-market usage of existing blockchains and cryptocurrencies has been hindered by their volatility and lack of scalability, which have, so far, made them poor stores of value and mediums of exchange," Facebook remarked in a June, 2019 white paper announcing its Libra token. "Some projects have also aimed to disrupt the existing system and bypass regulation as opposed to innovating on compliance and regulatory fronts to improve the effectiveness of anti-money laundering,"[196] Facebook observed. At summer solstice, 2020, John McAfee[197] launched Ghost affording anonymity across wallet and exchange.[198]

Amplifying Dorsey's 2018 reservations, President Donald J. Trump weighed in on July 11, 2019:

Donald J. Trump ✔
@realDonaldTrump

I am not a fan of Bitcoin and other Cryptocurrencies, which are not money, and whose value is highly volatile and based on thin air. Unregulated Crypto Assets can facilitate unlawful behavior, including drug trade and other illegal activity....

8:15 PM · Jul 11, 2019 · Twitter for iPhone

28.8K Retweets and comments   **66.9K** Likes

    18.8K   28.8K   66.9K

Show replies

Donald J. Trump ✔ @realDonaldTrump · Jul 11, 2019
....Similarly, Facebook Libra's "virtual currency" will have little standing or dependability. If Facebook and other companies want to become a bank, they must seek a new Banking Charter and become subject to all Banking Regulations, just like other Banks, both National...

    1.7K   10.5K   43K

Show replies

Donald J. Trump ✔ @realDonaldTrump · Jul 11, 2019
...and International. We have only one real currency in the USA, and it is stronger than ever, both dependable and reliable. It is by far the most dominant currency anywhere in the World, and it will always stay that way. It is called the United States Dollar!

    5.3K   10.8K   46.6K

KNOWN living contracts and immutable records address these concerns and obsolesce these reservations. If one were to embrace the motor vehicle metaphor of the Known Paradigm, immutable records document living contracts data frames, data incentives, data marketplaces and bit coins powered by top speed distributed ledger networks. Each and every vehicle sustains and maintains retrievable, indisputable records. A firm like Ripple[199], innovating an Internet of Value[200], could turbo-charge growth if it were to adopt and integrate KNOWN efficiencies and efficacies. Similarly, Square could boost its business volumes and asset value of its publicly traded digital wallet accounts.[201]

If one were to embrace an architectural metaphor, immutable records document each and every architectural element: site; that is, individuals, enterprises and institutions; transparency; that is, intent (choice), opportunity (means) and data quality; gravity, that is, the risk and monetary values. Immutable records ground and clarify each and all individual, enterprise and institution transaction from origination through maturity.

By so doing, the Known Paradigm clarifies risks, exposes frauds and suppresses crimes[202] like those fouling $600 T derivatives, commercial paper, repossession, and money markets of the 21st century unit decade and 1980's, all ripe for a fresh go with bitcoins and block chains.

In thinking to address supply chain challenges following the 2020 Coronavirus pandemic, the Known Paradigm is timely yielding transparency of "the common truth" latent in blockchains.[203]

Known Paradigm efficiencies and efficacies yield distinctly for digital currencies. Many digital currencies rely on intermediaries. Paradigm capabilities create trust for intermediaries so markets can clear and grow. "A high-level task force is currently examining the pros and cons of introducing a digital currency, which could be used by intermediaries or even by citizens through their electronic devices (such as smartphones or tablets) for their day-to-day spending needs. However, our analysis of the opportunities and challenges of central bank digital currencies – which will consider the experience of the COVID-19 crisis – should not discourage or crowd out market-led initiatives aimed at introducing private electronic means of payment with similar features in terms of user needs," the European Central Bank observed in April, 2020.[204]

Known Paradigm efficiencies and efficacies ground exchange traded funds by expediting and rationalizing secondary markets. By clarifying the risk and monetary values of assets in real time and near real time, Known Paradigm capabilities rationalize secondary market risk to expedite investor purchases of individual ETF shares in secondary markets. This is important due to primary market doldrums.[205]

 "An authorized participant that purchases a creation unit of ETF shares directly from the ETF deposits with the ETF a "basket" of securities and other assets identified by the ETF that day, and then receives the creation unit of ETF shares in return for those assets, the Securities & Exchange Commission observes. "The basket is generally representative of the ETF's portfolio, and together with a cash balancing amount, it is equal in value to the aggregate net asset value ("NAV") of the ETF shares in the creation unit. After purchasing a creation unit, the authorized participant may hold the individual ETF shares, or sell some or all of them in secondary market transactions. Investors then purchase individual ETF shares in the secondary market. The redemption process is the reverse of the purchase process: the authorized participant redeems a creation unit of ETF shares for a basket of securities and other assets."[206]

To address these dynamics, the SEC "adopt[ed] amendments to Forms N-1A and N-8B-2 to eliminate certain disclosures that we believe are no longer necessary and to require ETFs that do not rely on rule 6c-11 to provide secondary market investors with disclosures regarding certain ETF trading and associated costs. For example, the form amendments will require such an ETF to provide median bid-ask spread information either on its website or in its prospectus. We believe these amendments will provide investors who purchase ETF shares in secondary market transactions with information to better understand the total costs of investing in an ETF."[207]

Known Paradigm power disclosures vastly better with real and near real time risk and monetary values of the underlying assets to support robust ETF secondary markets.

Think of Known Paradigm capabilities clearing ETF secondary markets as a contemporaneous expression of Bernard Cantor's pioneering of transparency with computer terminal displays and dedicated long lines though, necessarily, vastly more robust, efficient and efficacious.

Known Paradigm capabilities now ground and orient 21st century Internet, wireless and wireline broadband, 5G, Internet of Things, cloud computing, artificial intelligence and machine learning research, development, deployment and commercialization by making indexical alphabets legible.

Contemplate the efficiencies and efficacies of individual-enterprise-and-institution-initiated revelations of the intent of searches and publications as well as notification of the searches and publications themselves. These would turbo-charge any artificial intelligence super-vacuum and information processor automating knowledge graphing.[208]

Capabilities afford speed by rewarding individuals, enterprises and institutions for indicating intent to transact verifiable assets. By mapping value and measuring risk to provide confidence over time and space, the innovations achieve vastly more than scoring the relevance of a search outcome to induce consumption.

Intent enables any and every individual, enterprise and institution transacting bitcoins over block chains to create wealth. The paradigm rationalizes bitcoin and block chain investment, research, development, deployment and commercialization. Functionalities accelerate authentication to reduce transaction costs parsing and verifying specific bitcoins and block chains coursing petabytes and zettabytes of data. Proof of bitcoin value can supplement and supersede proof of work. The innovations also police and suppress bitcoin and block chain fraud and money laundering.

Every individual, enterprise and institution can be themselves as fully as any and all wish to share and, by so doing, transfigure designations as 'users.'

All refine data and meta data to ground the 21st century gold standard by verifying transparent wealth and trustworthiness.

Each and all can re-embrace time as a friend through remunerative pleasure.

All own and control how to be known.

Afterword

The Sage sees all clearly all along.

"The general system of trade," Ralph Waldo Emerson observed in an 1841 lecture, "[is].... not measured by the exact laws of reciprocity, ...but is a system of distrust, of concealment...not giving but taking advantage...It is not that which a man delights to unlock to a noble friend; which he meditates on with joy and self-approval in his hour of love and aspiration; but rather what he then puts out of sight, only showing the brilliant result, and atoning for the manner of acquiring, by the manner of expending it. I do not charge the merchant or the manufacturer. The sins of our trade belong to no class, to no individual. One plucks, one distributes, one eats. Everybody partakes, everybody confesses, — with cap and knee volunteers his confession, yet none feels himself accountable. He did not create the abuse; he cannot alter it. What is he? an obscure private person who must get his bread. That is the vice — that no one feels himself called to act for man, but only as a fraction of man.... Our distrust is very expensive.... It is better to work on institutions by sun than by wind."[209]

Emerson made those observations following investor adoption of trusts and corporations as risk shielding vehicles to manage and deal with opacity resulting from Chief Justice Roger B. Taney preferencing innovation over contracts in Charles River Bridge v. Warren Bridge four years earlier (1837).[210]

In a withering dissent, Justice Joseph Story rejected Taney's the majority rationale and defended contracts. "[W]e have been told at the argument, that this very charter is a restriction upon the legislative power; that it is in derogation of the rights and interests of the state, and the people; that it tends to promote monopolies and exclusive privileges; and that it will interpose an insuperable barrier to the progress of improvement. Now, upon every one of these propositions, which are assumed, and not proved (emphasis supplied), I entertain a directly opposite opinion; and if I did not, I am not prepared to admit the conclusion for which they are adduced...

I deny the very ground-work of the argument. This charter is not any restriction upon the legislative power; unless it be true, that because the legislature cannot grant again, what it has already granted, the legislative power is restricted. If so, then every grant of the public land is a restriction upon that power; a doctrine, that has never yet been established, nor (so far as I know) ever contended for. Every grant of a franchise is, so far as that grant extends, necessarily exclusive; and cannot be resumed or interfered with. All the learned judges in the state court admitted, that the franchise of Charles River bridge, whatever it be, could not be resumed or interfered with. The legislature could not recall its grant, or destroy it. It is a contract, whose obligation cannot be constitutionally impaired."[211]

KNOWN living contractsTM and immutable records can now deploy transparency as a network effect. This powers reciprocity and advantage giving in 21st century Internet commerce and communications. In these ways, KNOWN capabilities embody solutions for distrust, concealment and advantage taking as Emerson so presciently foresaw.

KNOWN living contractsTM are more than merely smart. They are immutably recorded, living documents. Parties and counterparties can address and negotiate contract terms and conditions readily and easily with confidence of full records of any changes. These efficacies and efficiencies are indispensable to flourishing 21st century cryptocurrencies and bitcoins. This new paradigm's robust architecture delivers real time and near real time prices, values, terms and conditions. These are all documented at the exact points in time parties and counterparties transact contracts. This affords transparent market participation and administration. In these ways, KNOWN innovations freshly animate and vindicate Justice Story's cornerstone contract convictions.

"They should own who can administer," Emerson observed in Wealth (1860); "not they who hoard and conceal; not they who, the greater proprietors they are, are only the greater beggars, but they whose work carves out work for more, opens a path for all. For he is the rich man in whom the people are rich, and he is the poor man in whom the people are poor: and how to give all access to the masterpieces of art and nature, is the problem of civilization."[212]

In many ways, the existing Advertising Paradigm protracts this civilizational problem through advantage taking, concealment and distrust. It is as analogous to Restoration England, that stretch of English history from the coronation of Charles II in 1660 to the Hanoverian ascendency in 1714, as it is to the Venetian Republic. Concentration of wealth in finance capital and information technology has yielded comparable wealth inequalities.

William Penn is exact when he observes that "of old time the Nobility and Gentry spent their Estates in the Country, and that kept the people in it; and their Servants married and sate at easy Rents under their Masters' favor, which peopled the place: Now the Great men (too much loving the Town and resorting to London) draw many people thither to attend them, who either don't marry; or if they do, they pine away their small gains in some petty Shop; for there are so many, they prey upon one another."[213]

Until the coronavirus and civil unrest, all one need do is substitute contemporary New York, Seattle, Portland or San Francisco for Restoration London or baroque Venice and vast numbers of individuals, enterprises and institutions competing with each other with Internet commerce.

To be sure, the Advertising Paradigm affords opportunities, but wealth distributions are wholly analogous to those of Restoration England and the Venetian Republic.

By contrast, the Known Paradigm addresses the civilizational problem of wealth by originating intent as a fresh network element. This affords transparency as a fresh network effect to power Internet and 21st century commerce and communications.

APPENDIX I

Select Network, Internet, Content, Operating System revenues, 2019

Network Operators

AT&T: 181.2B

https://about.att.com/story/2020/2019_earnings.html

Charter/Spectrum Communications: 45.7B

https://www.macrotrends.net/stocks/charts/CHTR/charter-communications/revenue

Comcast: 108.9B

https://www.statista.com/statistics/273560/comcast-corporations-annual-revenue/

Verizon: 131.8B

https://www.macrotrends.net/stocks/charts/VZ/verizon/revenue

Content Producers

Disney: 69.5B

https://thewaltdisneycompany.com/the-walt-disney-company-reports-fourth-quarter-and-full-year-earnings-for-fiscal-2019/

Netflix: 20.1B

https://www.macrotrends.net/stocks/charts/NFLX/netflix/revenue

Retail Sales

Amazon: 280.5B

https://www.macrotrends.net/stocks/charts/AMZN/amazon/revenue

Social Media

Facebook: 70.7B

https://www.statista.com/statistics/268604/annual-revenue-of-facebook/

Search

Alphabet (Google): 161.9B

https://www.macrotrends.net/stocks/charts/GOOG/alphabet/revenue

Portable Connectivity Equipment/Retail Sales

Apple: 260.2B

https://www.apple.com/newsroom/2019/10/apple-reports-fourth-quarter-results/

Operating Systems

Microsoft: 125.8B

https://www.microsoft.com/investor/reports/ar19/index.html

ACKNOWLEDGEMENTS

Thanks to Andrew McCollister Fukuzawa Donahue, Rose Gwendolyn Donahue and the late Thomas S. Kuhn for inspiration, Rowan University Campbell Library and Conshohocken Free Library librarians, Jack Amon, Philip Y. Braginsky, Esq., Vayia Karavangelas, Carter Laborde, Vito Mattaliano, Jake Morsillo, Neal Nowakowski, David M. Rowe, Ph.D., Stephen Schueren, an exceptionally, fine man, Gary A. Smith, Esq., Emily Weyman and Denise Williams.

Art and graphic design by Vito Mattaliano.

Admiration for Constance and Michael Erlangers' and Michael Harold's inventive methods motivated this research and writing.

I am an advisor to Marketcore, a KNOWN predecessor company.

Any and all errors are mine.

ENDNOTES

1 See Masayoshi Amamiya, Deputy Governor of the Bank of Japan, "Central Bank Digital Currency and the future of payment and settlement systems," Future of Payments Forum, Tokyo, February 27, 2020 for nonbank payment service providers and digital currencies, https://www.bis.org/review/r200306a.pdf, and The Wall Street Journal, January 14, 2020 for the planned obsolescence of cookies.
"Their [nonbank payment service providers'] aim is not only to improve the convenience of customers, but also to seek to expand their own ecosystem via network effects by inducing customers to use other relevant businesses NBPSPs offer," Amamiya observes. "This strategy is called "Data-Network-Activity (DNA). "In the past, making payments for purchases, in other words, using money, meant an exchange of certain amount of economic value. Nowadays, it also means an exchange of relevant data on who has purchased what, when and where. In some cases, the exchanged data could be data that the web advertisement has just been viewed, but nothing has been purchased. Therefore, when we explore the future of the payment and settlement systems, it becomes more vital to discuss issues concerning the protection and effective use of personal data, he forecautions.
Amamiya articulates the generational insight: "[M]oney and data will become more closely linked."

2 Warner & Hawley Introduce Bill to Force Social Media Companies to Disclose How They Are Monetizing User Data
  https://www.warner.senate.gov/public/index.cfm/2019/6/warner-hawley-introduce-bill-to-force-social-media-companies-to-disclose-how-they-are-monetizing-user-data

3 The Verge, October 17, 2019.

4 Team Warren, Medium, March 8, 2019. https://medium.com/@teamwarren/heres-how-we-can-break-up-big-tech-9ad9e0da324c

5 Remarks by Secretary of Commerce Wilbur Ross at Oxford Union in Oxford, England. https://www.commerce.gov/news/speeches/2020/02/remarks-secretary-commerce-wilbur-ross-oxford-union-oxford-england

6 Adam Goodman, "How Obama just endorsed Trump," The Hill, May 28, 2020.

7 "Frances Fox Piven on Why Protesters Must "Defend Their Ability to Exercise Disruptive Power" AN INTERVIEW WITH FRANCES FOX PIVEN, The Jacobin, June 17, 2020.

8 "NYC Doctor Claims Covid 19 is not what they say it is," https://www.youtube.com/watch?v=0yrCjsaZKg8&fbclid=IwAR0kh6_Eo1exx-188Ani2AqXtnyMNoZcnBTxYz4TnuNPcWCzf4ZPYd_iDsA

9 Peter Apps, "Coronavirus unleashes economic warfare," Japan Times, March 10, 2020.

10   This is how much the coronavirus will cost the world's economy, according to the UN https://www.weforum.org/agenda/2020/03/coronavirus-covid-19-cost-economy-2020-un-trade-economics-pandemic/

11 Siegfrid Alegado, "Global Cost of Coronavirus May Reach $4.1 Trillion, ADB Says" April 2, 2020, https://www.bloomberg.com/news/articles/2020-04-03/global-cost-of-coronavirus-could-reach-4-1-trillion-adb-says

12 Steve Goldstein, "Pandemic could cost global economy $82 trillion in depression scenario," Marketwatch, May 20, 2020 https://www.marketwatch.com/story/today-in-scary-numbers-pandemic-could-cost-global-economy-82-trillion-2020-05-19?mod=home-page

13 Richard N. Velotta, "Macao gaming revenue hits record low in June," Las Vegas Review-Journal, July 2, 2020 https://www.reviewjournal.com/business/casinos-gaming/macao-gaming-revenue-hits-record-low-in-june-2066614/

14 Prince Harry Sends Message to Invictus Competitors on Day of Cancelled Opening Ceremony, May 10, 2020 https://www.youtube.com/watch?v=gbhccEmc-t0

15 Jerome H. Powell, Chairman, Federal Reserve Board, Speech, Peterson Institute for International Economics, Washington, D.C., May 13, 2020 https://www.federalreserve.gov/newsevents/speech/powell20200513a.htm

16 The Employment Situation, Bureau of Labor Statistics, https://www.bls.gov/news.release/pdf/empsit.pdf

17 "Swamped Bankruptcy Courts Threaten US Recovery," https://www.ft.com/content/14b07c0e-95e3-11ea-af4b-499244625ac4?fbclid=IwAR3IId4irwHLevwfUH3tbmuduE_voNdLLI0Ih2Xb2gdBe00nfHtiOBignfw

18 Former Fed vice chair Alan Blinder on public debt and the market surge, May 18, 2020 https://www.youtube.com/watch?v=1pwZC_SAXYg

19 Steven Longenecker, Our Upside Down Coronavirus World, May 2020, https://americanconsequences.com/our-upside-down-coronavirus-world-2/

20 Thomas E. Johnsen, "Supplier involvement in new product development and innovation: taking stock and looking to the future." Journal of Purchasing & Supply Management, Volume 15, 2009, 187-197.

21   Charlotte Edmond, "3 challenges in creating a coronavirus vaccine – and how they are being overcome," May 14, Formative Content, WEF, https://www.weforum.org/agenda/2020/05/coronavirus-covid-19-vaccine-industry/?utm_source=sfmc&utm_medium=email&utm_campaign=2719847_Age nda_weekly-22May2020&utm_term=&emailType=Newsletter

22 U.S. Department of Justice Antitrust Division Update 2020
https://www.justice.gov/file/1280196/download

23   Live: President Trump Speech at Ypsilanti, Michigan Ford Components Plant
 https://rsbnetwork.com/2020/05/live-president-trump-speech-at-ypsilanti-michigan-ford-components-plant/

24 Patrick Tan, Deglobalization & Digital Currencies, Medium, June 5, 2020 https://medium.com/the-capital/deglobalization-digital-currencies-3774f2ae045b

25   Yan Xiao and Ziyang Fan, "10 technology trends to watch in the COVID-19 pandemic," WEF Industry Agenda, April 27, 2020
https://www.weforum.org/agenda/2020/04/10-technology-trends-coronavirus-covid19-pandemic-robotics-telehealth/?utm_source=sfmc&utm_medium=email&utm_term=&utm_conte nt=42853&utm_id=50180981-ce02-45c4-9b2c-2c4934dc3ff8&sfmc_id=358147975&sfmc_activityid=c1721a48-bd6f-4f94-bb01-e7019f5b68ce&utm_source=sfmc&utm_medium=email&utm_campaign=2716 919_StrategicIntelligenceWeeklyV2-3&utm_term=&emailType=Strategic%20Intelligence%20Newsletter&sk=MD AxMFgwMDAwNEt2RzlBUUFW

26 "Twitter generally actions Tweets that violate our rules.
However, we recognize that sometimes it may be in the public interest to allow people to view Tweets that would otherwise be taken down. We consider content to be in the public interest if it directly contributes to understanding or discussion of a matter of public concern.
At present, we limit exceptions to one critical type of public-interest content—Tweets from elected and government officials—given the significant public interest in knowing and being able to discuss their actions and statements.
As a result, in rare instances, we may choose to leave up a Tweet from an elected or government official that would otherwise be taken down. Instead we will place it behind a notice providing context about the rule violation that allows people to click through to see the Tweet. Placing a Tweet behind this notice also limits the ability to engage with the Tweet through likes, Retweets, or sharing on Twitter, and makes sure the Tweet isn't algorithmically recommended by Twitter. These actions are meant to limit the Tweet's reach while maintaining the public's ability to view and discuss it."

27 https://twitter.com/realdonaldtrump/status/1266231100172615680

28 https://www.law.cornell.edu/uscode/text/47/230

29 Executive Order on Preventing Online Censorship INFRASTRUCTURE & TECHNOLOGY, May 28, 2020 https://www.whitehouse.gov/presidential-actions executive-order-preventing-onl19ine-censorship/

30 https://twitter.com/gopleader/status/1275512945364152322?lang=en

31 Cameron F. Kerry and John B. Morris, "Why data ownership is the wrong approach to protecting privacy," Brookings, June 26, 2019 https://www.brookings.edu/blog/techtank/2019/06/26/why-data-ownership-is-the-wrong-approach-to-protecting-privacy/

32 Michel Feher, Rated Agency: Investee Politics in a Speculative Age, 2018; Yuval Noah Harari, "Dataism Is Our New God," New Perspectives Quarterly, Volume 34, Number 2, May, 2017, Homo Deus, A Brief History of Tomorrow (2015).
"The basic idea of dataism is a shift in authority. Previously, authority resided above the clouds and descended down to the pope, the king or the czar. Then for the last two or three centuries, authority came down from the clouds and took up residence in people's hearts. Your feelings became the highest source of authority. The emotions of the voters in a democracy, not his or her rationality, became the number one authority in politics. In the economics of the consumer society, it is the feelings of the customer that drive every market. The feelings of the individual are the prime authority in ethics. "If it feels good, do it" is the basic ethical ideal of humanism." "So, authority came down from the clouds, moved to the human heart and now authority is shifting back to the Google cloud and the Microsoft cloud. Data, and the ability to analyze data, is the new source of authority. If you have a problem in life, whether it is what to study, whom to marry or whom to vote for, you don't ask God above or your feelings inside, you ask Google or Facebook. If they have enough data on you, and enough computing power, they know what you feel already and why you feel that way. Based on that, they can allegedly make much better decisions on your behalf than you can on your own," Harari observes in the NPQ article.

33 The Telecommunications Act of 1996
https://transition.fcc.gov/Reports/tcom1996.pdf

34 C.E. Shannon, "A Mathematical Theory of Communication," The Bell System Technical Journal, Vol. 27, pp. 379–423, 623–656, July, October, 1948
http://people.math.harvard.edu/~ctm/home/text/others/shannon/entropy/entropy.pdf

35 Gordon E. Moore, "Cramming more components onto integrated circuits," Electronics, Volume 38, Number 8, April 19, 1965. https://newsroom.intel.com/wp-content/uploads/sites/11/2018/05/moores-law-electronics.pdf

36 Ronald A. Howard, "Information Value Theory," IEEE Transactions on Systems Science and Cybernetics (Volume:2, Issue:1, August, 1966
https://ieeexplore.ieee.org/abstract/document/4082064

37 Ibid. https://ieeexplore.ieee.org/abstract/document/4082064

38 Paul W. Litchfield, Industrial Voyage My Life as An Industrial Lieutenant, (1954), p.133-5.

39 "Mario Botta on Modernism, Technology and Main Principles of His Work," https://www.archdaily.com/919544/mario-botta-on-modernism-technology-and-main-principles-of-his-work

40 Eugene F. Fama and Burton G. Malkiel, "Efficient Capital Markets: A Review of Theory and Empirical Work," Journal of Finance Volume 25, Issue 2, 1970. https://onlinelibrary.wiley.com/doi/abs/10.1111/j.1540-6261.1970.tb00518.x

41 Dev Kundaliya, "Internet governance body RIPE opposes Chinese proposal to change core internet protocols," Computing, April 24, 2020
  https://www.computing.co.uk/news/4014383/internet-governance-body-ripe-opposes-chinese-proposal-change-core-internet-protocols

42 Marco Hogewoning, "Do We Need a New IP?" "The most problematic and dangerous part of the proposal is not the technology, but the fundamental beliefs behind it, which represent a departure from the Internet's fundamental values of openness, transparency and putting the end user in control," Marco Hogewoning, RIPE NCC Manager Public Policy and Internet Governance, observes in a thoughtful April, 2020 blog post. "The current Internet was not so much designed as grown over time and often only documented ex post. The multi-stakeholder model wasn't invented; it was the best description we had of how things had been working for decades already. It served a purpose in documenting how it was different from the traditional multilateral decision-making processes (such as those still practised by the ITU)." https://labs.ripe.net/Members/marco_hogewoning/do-we-need-a-new-ip "Staff from Huawei and Futurewei, its R&D branch, have made it clear on several occasions that they see New IP as an opportunity to redesign the governance model into a top-down structure," he points out. "This is the case with the design and standardization efforts, but also comes through in the network's envisioned functioning. Despite the many claims of taking a decentralized approach, forwarding and access to the network itself would be controlled from centralized authorities who, for instance, would be able to signal subordinate network elements to block a particular data flow. This is much more of a fundamental shift than it first appears to be, as it would give control to the core of the network instead of leaving it to the end points, as we mostly do on the Internet today." https://labs.ripe.net/Members/marco_hogewoning/do-we-need-a-new-ip

43 Naomi Klein, "Coronavirus Capitalism – and How To Beat It," The Intercept, March 16 2020. https://theintercept.com/2020/03/16/coronavirus-capitalism/

44 Ibid. https://theintercept.com/2020/03/16/coronavirus-capitalism/
45 Dr Johnny Ryan testimony. Understanding the Digital Advertising Ecosystem and the Impact of Data Privacy and Competition Policy. Senate Judiciary Committee https://www.judiciary.senate.gov/imo/media/doc/Ryan%20Testimony.pdf

46 Abi Gibbons, "Time for change and transparency in programmatic advertising," May 6, 2020 https://www.isba.org.uk/news/time-for-change-and-transparency-in-programmatic-advertising/

47 Ibid. https://www.isba.org.uk/news/time-for-change-and-transparency-in-programmatic-advertising/

48 Charles Mi, "As cookies fade, brands must create a robust identity strategy," July 22,2020 https://www.warc.com/newsandopinion/opinion/as-cookies-fade-brands-must-create-a-robust-identity-strategy/3735

49 FT Partners, "The Rise of Challenger Banks: Are the Apps Taking Over?" https://www.ftpartners.com/fintech-research/challenger-banks

50 Kevin Wack, "Community Bankers Alarmed After Big Bank Backtrack on faster payments pricing," The American Banker, April 10, 2019

51 See Dodd Frank Act https://www.congress.gov/111/crpt/hrpt517/CRPT-111hrpt517.pdf

52 Liam Tung, "Details on 80 million US households exposed by unprotected cloud database," ZDNet, April 30, 2019

53 See David Marchese, "The Disruptive World of Edward Norton," The New York Times Magazine, Oct. 7, 2019. https://www.gq.com/story/edward-norton-motherless-brooklyn-profile

54 Final Rule, Exchange Traded Funds, SECURITIES AND EXCHANGE COMMISSION 17 CFR Parts 210, 232, 239, 270, and 274 [Release Nos. 33-10695; IC-33646; File No. S7-15-18] RIN 3235-AJ60.

55 Lael Brainard, Cryptocurrencies, Digital Currencies, and Distributed Ledger Technologies: What Are We Learning? Decoding Digital Currency Conference sponsored by the Federal Reserve Bank of San Francisco, San Francisco, California, May 15, 2018. See also Lael Brainard, An Update on Digital Currencies, Federal Reserve Board and Federal Reserve Bank of San Francisco's Innovation Office Hours, San Francisco, California, August 13, 2020 https://www.federalreserve.gov/newsevents/speech/brainard20200813a.htm

56 See, for instance, North Carolina Flood Risk Information System, https://fris.nc.gov/fris/Home.aspx?ST=NC

57 J. Michael Luttig and David B. Rivkin, "Lawsuits Needn't Block Recovery," The Wall Street Journal, May 21, 2020.

58 Jann Swanson, "CFPB Warns Servicers and Lenders to Adhere to CARES Act,"

Mortgage Daily News, Jun 5 2020.

59 O'Kelley Statement, Senate Judiciary Committee, https://www.judiciary.senate.gov/imo/media/doc/O'Kelley%20Testimony.pdf

60 Rob Williams, "How Publishers Can Thrive As Third-Party Cookies Fade," Publishing Insider, February 11, 2020.

61 Reddit cofounder asked to be replaced by a black board member. The company listened, CNN Business, https://www.cnn.com/videos/business/2020/06/05/alexis-ohanian-reddit-resign-orig-zw.cnn

62 "What's the Matter with Eastern Kentucky?", The New York Times Magazine, June 29, 2014 https://www.nytimes.com/2014/06/29/magazine/whats-the-matter-with-eastern-kentucky.html?emc=eta1&_r=0

63 Frank Newport, Race Relations as the Nation's Most Important Problem, June 19, 2020 https://news.gallup.com/opinion/polling-matters/312875/race-relations-nation-important-problem.aspx

64 Neil Richards and Woodrow Hartzog, "Taking Trust Seriously in Privacy Law," 19 STAN.TECH. L.REV. 431 (2016) https://www-cdn.law.stanford.edu/wp-content/uploads/2017/11/Taking-Trust-Seriously-in-Privacy-Law.pdf

65 The Oxford English Dictionary typifies "to publish information about (a person (now rare), thing, circumstance, or event) so as to attract public attention; (b) to describe or present (a product, service, or the like) in order to promote sales… by, in, on the medium specified (as a journal, radio, television, etc.)."

66 Thomas S. Kuhn, The Structure of Scientific Revolutions, http://www.bard.edu/library/arendt/pdfs/Kuhn_ScientificRevolutions.pdf

67 Ibid.

68 https://www.forbes.com/profile/michael-bloomberg/?list=rtb/#361a19c01417

69 Soshana Zuboff, "Surveillance Capitalism and the Challenge of Collective Action," New Labor Forum, January, 2019. https://newlaborforum.cuny.edu/2019/01/22/surveillance-capitalism/

70 https://www.publicaffairsbooks.com/titles/shoshana-zuboff/the-age-of-surveillance-capitalism/9781610395694/

71 See endnote 69.

72 See endnote 69.

73 Paul W. Litchfield, Industrial Voyage My Life as an Industrial Lieutenant (1954).

74 Ibid.

75 https://wwnorton.com/college/history/america-essential-learning/docs/FWTaylor-Scientific_Mgmt-1911.pdf

76 "Management, as distinct from ownership, was something new in the business world [and] grew out of the increasing size of business units. Business is the joint effort of capital and labor to create goods society needs. To get the best results for both, the interests of both must be kept in balance. That is management's responsibility, to both, not to capital alone." p. 21
"It did not seem to me a good thing for a democratic country, where everyone was entitled to vote, to bring in immigrants, work them long hours at menial tasks, pay them little, call them 'Hunkies,' 'Dagos,' and 'Polacks,' deny them a decent living and the opportunity to get ahead. Men were entitled to a better break. I was convinced also that men who were well paid and well treated would turn out a better product, be worth more money," Litchfield observes in Industrial Voyage, p.72-73.

77 Litchfield, Industrial Voyage, p. 108-109.

78 Thomas Piketty, Wealth in the 21st Century (2014), https://www.hup.harvard.edu/catalog.php?isbn=9780674430006

79 Jonathan D. Fisher and David S. Johnson, "Inequality and Mobility over the Past Half Century using Income, Consumption and Wealth," NBER, 2020. https://www.nber.org/chapters/c14444.pdf

80 Richard H. Steckel and Carolyn M. Moehling, "Wealth Inequality Trends in Industrializing New England: New Evidence and Tests of Competing Hypotheses, NBER Historical Working Paper, 2000. https://www.nber.org/papers/h0122

81 Conor Grant, "How teenage hackers became tech's go-to bounty hunters," The Hustle, April 26, 2019. https://thehustle.co/teenage-hackers-bug-bounty/

82 Facebook v. Rankwave, Superior Court of the State of California for the County of San Mateo, May 10, 2019 https://techcrunch.com/wp-content/uploads/2019/05/TechCrunch-Facebook-Rankwave-Lawsuit.pdf

83 George Gilder, Life After Google The Fall of Big Data and the Rise of the Blockchain Economy, 2018 https://www.regnery.com/9781621575764/life-after-google/

84 Ross Wilkers, "Former Northrop cyber business BluVector bought by Comcast," Washington Technology, March 4, 2019. https://washingtontechnology.com/articles/2019/03/04/bluvector-comcast-sale.aspx

85 James Bourne, "Comcast acquires AI-powered cybersecurity technology developer BluVector," AINEWS, March 6, 2019 https://artificialintelligence-

news.com/2019/03/06/comcast-acquires-ai-powered-cybersecurity-technology-developer-bluevector/

86 Johnny Ryan, A summary of the ICO report on RTB – and what happens next, June 26, 2019 https://brave.com/ico-adtech-update-rtb/

87 See endnote 82.

88 Facebook for Developers 2020-02-03 Endpoint Deprecations https://developers.facebook.com/docs/graph-api/changelog/2020-02-03-endpoint-deprecations

89 District of Columbia v. Facebook, Superior Court of the District of Columbia Civil Division, March 22, 2019 https://www.documentcloud.org/documents/5777489-Search-Page-3-1.html?fbclid=IwAR1INJzK4r-Y088pTwXTKothKNhr_jUiUAkDXcNB8mXSfqFABJtUN4wL3eo

90 Renee DiResta, "Computational Propaganda If You Make It Trend, You Make It True," The Yale Review, https://yalereview.yale.edu/computational-propaganda

91 Federal Trade Commission, "FTC Imposes $5 Billion Penalty and Sweeping New Privacy Restrictions on Facebook" July 24, 2019. https://www.ftc.gov/news-events/press-releases/2019/07/ftc-imposes-5-billion-penalty-sweeping-new-privacy-restrictions

92 The Federal Trade Commission, In the Matter concerning Facebook Corporation, FILE NO 092 3184 AGREEMENT CONTAINING CONSENT ORDER https://www.ftc.gov/sites/default/files/documents/cases/2011/11/111129facebookagree.pdf

93 PREPARED STATEMENT OF THE FEDERAL TRADE COMMISSION: OVERSIGHT OF THE FEDERAL TRADE COMMISSION Before the COMMITTEE ON ENERGY AND COMMERCE SUBCOMMITTEE ON CONSUMER PROTECTION AND COMMERCE UNITED STATES HOUSE OF REPRESENTATIVES WASHINGTON, DC MAY 8, 2019 https://www.ftc.gov/system/files/documents/public_statements/1519212/p180101_house_ec_oversight_testimony_may_8_2019.pdf

94 United States v. Facebook, UNITED STATES DISTRICT COURT FOR THE DISTRICT OF COLUMBIA, Case No. 19-cv-2184, July 24, 2019. https://www.ftc.gov/system/files/documents/cases/182_3109_facebook_complaint_filed_7-24-19.pdf

95 FACEBOOK v. ONEAUDIENCE LLC CASE NO.: 3:20-cv-01461 UNITED STATES DISTRICT COURT NORTHERN DISTRICT OF CALIFORNIA SAN FRANCISCO DIVISION, February 27, 2020 https://www.courtlistener.com/recap/gov.uscourts.cand.356034/gov.uscourts.cand.356034.1.0.pdf

96 Wendy Davis, "Facebook Sues Mobile Analytics Company OneAudience Over Data Mining," Digital News Daily, February 27, 2020 https://www.mediapost.com/publications/article/347752/facebook-sues-mobile-analytics-company-oneaudience.html

97 Josh Constine, "Facebook pivots to what it wishes it was Zuckerberg gets aspirational," Tech Crunch, May 1, 2019 https://techcrunch.com/2019/05/01/aspirationbook/?guccounter=1

98 Nick Statt, "Facebook is redesigning its core app around the two parts people actually like to use," The Verge, Apr 30, 2019 https://www.theverge.com/2019/4/30/18523265/facebook-events-groups-redesign-news-feed-features-f8-2019

99 Facebook Community Standards https://www.facebook.com/communitystandards/dangerous_individuals_organizations

100 Simon Van Zuylen-Wood, "MEN ARE SCUM": INSIDE FACEBOOK'S WAR ON HATE SPEECH," Vanity Fair, March, 2019. https://www.vanityfair.com/news/2019/02/men-are-scum-inside-facebook-war-on-hate-speech

101 https://www.randomdecisionmaker.com/

102 "You Will Wish You Watched This Before You Started Using Social Media | The Twisted Truth" https://www.youtube.com/watch?v=PmEDAzqswh8

103 Kate Whiting, "The world is getting angrier, according to a new poll," World Economic Forum, Global Agenda, May 1, 2019. https://www.weforum.org/agenda/2019/05/worried-angry-and-sad-5-things-to-know-about-how-miserable-the-world-is/

104 Marcia W. DiStaso and Tina McCorkindale, THE SCIENCE OF INFLUENCE: HOW SOCIAL MEDIA AFFECTS DECISION MAKING IN THE HEALTHCARE, TRAVEL, RETAIL AND FINANCIAL INDUSTRIES, December 11, 2017 https://instituteforpr.org/science-influence-social-media-affects-decision-making-healthcare-travel-retail-financial-industries/

105 Liam Tung, "Programming languages: Developers reveal most loved, most loathed, what pays best," ZDNet, April 9, 2019 https://www.zdnet.com/article/programming-languages-developers-reveal-most-loved-most-loathed-what-pays-best/?ftag=TRE-03-10aaa6b&bhid=28493564473397578750343099000497

106 "Clojure embodies and demonstrates the continued viability of the Lisp idea, including the importance of a simple core, direct use of data, extension via libraries, and dynamic typing in delivering flexibility and reducing coupling," Rich Hickey observes in "A History of Clojure," ACM Program. Lang., Vol. 4, No. HOPL, Article 71, June, 2020.

107 Billy Jones & Ernest Hare – "Henry's Made A Lady Out Of Lizzie," 1928 https://www.youtube.com/watch?v=ow8ZRF4vjD4

108 Allen Wirfs-Brock and Brendan Eich, "JavaScript: The First 20 Years," Proc. ACM Program. Lang. 4, HOPL, Article 77 (June 2020), 189 pages. https://doi.org/10.1145/3386327 https://dl.acm.org/doi/pdf/10.1145/3386327

109 eMarketer Editors, "Google Ad Revenues to Drop for the First Time Facebook and Amazon shares will grow, June 23, 2020, eMarketer https://www.emarketer.com/content/google-ad-revenues-drop-first-time?ecid=NL1009&fbclid=IwARIzSYyEJ0qskvEcdW5C03gQ31UzrTjrqVFg9SqY35D1qd1Brrw24cs03DI

110 Billy Murray – "The Little Ford Rambled Right Along" https://www.youtube.com/watch?v=hUzxcApgdUc

111 Matthew Ingram, "How did the digital giants get so big, and what should we do about it?" CJR, April 16, 2020. https://www.cjr.org/the_media_today/always-day-one.php?utm_source=CJR+Daily+News&utm_campaign=e119d8992e-EMAIL_CAMPAIGN_2018_10_31_05_02_COPY_01&utm_medium=email&utm_term=0_9c93f57676-e119d8992e-174377885&mc_cid=e119d8992e&mc_eid=97627f6796

112 Harper Neidig, "Facebook expects $3B-$5B fine over Cambridge Analytica," The Hill, April, 24, 2019. https://thehill.com/policy/technology/440514-facebook-says-it-expects-3b-5b-fine-over-cambridge-analytica-scandal

113 David S. Platt, Why Software Sucks...and What You Can Do About It https://www.amazon.com/gp/product/0321466756/ref=as_li_tl?ie=UTF8&camp=1789&creative=9325&creativeASIN=0321466756&linkCode=as2&tag=rollingthun01-20&linkId=CZVH2NMYBIMACAEB

114 Welcome to Windows 10 https://www.neowin.net/news/welcome-to-the-windows-10-era

115 Microsoft Announces Project Mu to promote Firmware as a Service https://www.neowin.net/news/microsoft-announces-project-mu-to-promote-firmware-as-a-service/

116 Microsoft Build 2019 // Vision Keynote + Imagine Cup World Championship, May 6, 2019 https://www.youtube.com/watch?v=ZbpjLchrYgw

117 Jeff Bezos is selling $1B of Amazon stock per year to fund Blue Origin as a separate company cultivating low earth orbit travel experiences, space settlement and service and product delivery, news reports indicate. "In 2018, Jeff Bezos accumulated roughly $150,000 per minute, as his net worth grew by $78.5 billion that year. While health economists routinely decry doctors' salaries in the United States, almost no physician earns in a lifetime what Bezos accumulated in one day that year (about $213 million)," Frank Pasquale observed in Commonweal, June, 2020.
William Gates invested $10B in vaccine technologies and projected a 20:1 return on investment in 2019.

118 Maria Fusaro, Political Economies of Empire in the Early Modern Mediterranean The Decline of Venice and the Rise of England, 1450–1700, 2017 https://www.cambridge.org/be/academic/subjects/history/european-history-after-1450/political-economies-empire-early-modern-mediterranean-decline-venice-and-rise-england-14501700?format=PB

119 Code Civil des Francais https://gallica.bnf.fr/ark:/12148/bpt6k1061517/f3.image

120 Johnny Ryan, Understanding the Digital Advertising Ecosystem and the Impact of Data Privacy and Competition Policy, Senate Judiciary Committee https://www. judiciary.senate.gov/imo/media/doc/Ryan%20Testimony.pdf

121 Understanding the Digital Advertising Ecosystem and the Impact of Data Privacy and Competition Policy, May 21, 2019 https://www.judiciary.senate.gov/meetings/ understanding-the-digital-advertising-ecosystem-and-the-impact-of-data-privacy-and-competition-policy

122 Johnny Ryan, New data on GDPR enforcement agencies reveal why the GDPR is failing, March 27, 2020 https://brave.com/dpa-report-2020/

123 Imanol Arrieta-Ibarra, Leonard Goff, Diego Jimenez-Hernandez, Jaron Lanier, E. Glen Weyl, "Should We Treat Data as Labor? Moving beyond "Free," AEA Papers and Proceedings, Vol 108, May 2018, https://www.aeaweb.org/articles?id=10.1257/ pandp.20181003

124 Ibid.

125 Marc Bellemare, Will Dabney, Robert Dadashi, Adrien Taiga, Pablo Castro, Nicholas Roux, Dale Schuurmans, Dale, Tor Lattimore, Clare Lyle, A Geometric Perspective on Optimal Representations for Reinforcement Learning. (2019). https:// www.researchgate.net/publication/330777528_A_Geometric_Perspective_on_ Optimal_Representations_for_Reinforcement_Learning/citation/download

126 Ibid. https://arxiv.org/pdf/1901.11530.pdf

127 Alexey Dosovitskiy and Vladlen Koltun, "Learning to Act by Predicting the Future," Published as a conference paper at ICLR 2017 https://arxiv.org/pdf/1611.01779.pdf

128 Ibid.

129 Larry Dignan, "Top cloud providers 2019: AWS, Microsoft Azure, Google Cloud; IBM makes hybrid move; Salesforce dominates SaaS," ZDNet, August 15, 2019 https://www.zdnet.com/article/top-cloud-providers-2019-aws-microsoft-azure-google-cloud-ibm-makes-hybrid-move-salesforce-dominates-saas/?ftag=TRE-03-10aaa6b&bhid=28493564473397578750343099000497

130 James Surowieck, "Why Tesla Is Worth More Than GM," Technology Review, June 27, 2017, https://www.technologyreview.com/2017/06/27/150794/why-tesla-is-worth-more-than-gm/

131 Elizabeth Warren, "Here's how we can break up Big Tech," Medium, March 8, 2019 https://medium.com/@teamwarren/heres-how-we-can-break-up-big-tech-9ad9e0da324c

132 Catalin Cimpanu, "Dutch government report says Microsoft Office telemetry collection breaks GDPR," ZDNET, November 14, 2018, https://www.zdnet.com/article/dutch-government-report-says-microsoft-office-telemetry-collection-breaks-gdpr/

133 Joseph Stiglitz, People, Power, and Profits Progressive Capitalism for an Age of Discontent, https://wwnorton.com/books/People-Power-and-Profits

134 See Mathew Ingram, "How did the digital giants get so big, and what should we do about it?," Columbia Journalism Review, April 16, 2020. https://www.cjr.org/the_media_today/always-day-one.php?utm_source=CJR+Daily+News&utm_campaign=e119d8992e-EMAIL_CAMPAIGN_2018_10_31_05_02_COPY_01&utm_medium=email&utm_term=0_9c93f57676-e119d8992e-174377885&mc_cid=e119d8992e&mc_eid=97627f6796

135 Mark Zuckerberg, "The Internet needs new rules. Let's start in these four areas," The Washington Post, March 30, 2019. https://www.washingtonpost.com/opinions/mark-zuckerberg-the-internet-needs-new-rules-lets-start-in-these-four-areas/2019/03/29/9e6f0504-521a-11e9-a3f7-78b7525a8d5f_story.html

136 Ben Sasse, THEM Why We Hate Each Other--and How to Heal, 2018 https://us.macmillan.com/books/9781250193681

137 David M. Rowe, "Dangerous Adaptation," Transparency Times #35 March 2019 https://issuu.com/andyagathangelou/docs/transparency_times__35_march_2019

138 Chris Hughes, "It's Time to Break Up Facebook," The New York Times, May 9, 2019 https://www.nytimes.com/2019/05/09/opinion/sunday/chris-hughes-facebook-zuckerberg.html

139 Brendan Blumer, Keynote Address, June 1, 2019 Block One https://block.one/events/

140 https://brave.com/about/

141 https://twitter.com/brendaneich/status/1269313200127795201?lang=en

142 Facebook, 01 White Paper, https://libra.org/en-US/white-paper/#introduction

143 The Libra Association https://libra.org/en-US/association/

144 The Libra Association https://libra.org/en-US/association/#overview

145 Economics and the Libra Reserve https://libra.org/en-US/economics-and-the-reserve/#overview

146 The Libra Blockchain https://developers.libra.org/docs/the-libra-blockchain-paper

147 Alex Kantrowitz, Always Day One How The Tech Titans Plan to Stay On Top Forever https://www.penguinrandomhouse.com/books/607065/always-day-one-by-alex-kantrowitz/

148 See 134.

149 https://galley.cjr.org/public/conversations/-M4uBJ2xD4EueeXJ1AUK

150 Dipayan Ghosh, Terms of Disservice: How Silicone Valley is Destructive By Design https://www.brookings.edu/book/terms-of-disservice/

151 Theodore Schleifer, "Facebook and Twitter took down a Trump campaign video over copyright concerns, Vox, June 5, 2020 https://www.vox.com/recode/2020/6/5/21281787/twitter-trump-george-floyd-campaign-video-copyright

152 Jacob Rosenberg, "An Uprising Is Still Possible, Even if We Can't Meet in the Streets, Mother Jones, May 1, 2020 https://www.motherjones.com/politics/2020/05/an-uprising-is-still-possible-even-if-we-cant-meet-in-the-streets/

153 Alex Hern and Julia Carrie Wong, "Facebook employees hold virtual walkout over Mark Zuckerberg's refusal to act against Trump," The Guardian, June 1, 2020, https://www.theguardian.com/technology/2020/jun/01/facebook-workers-rebel-mark-zuckerberg-donald-trump

154 https://www.facebook.com/zuck/posts/10111985969467901

155 "For nonconformity the world whips you with its displeasure, Emerson observes in Self-Reliance. "And therefore a man must know how to estimate a sour face. The by-standers look askance on him in the public street or in the friend's parlour. If this aversation had its origin in contempt and resistance like his own, he might well go home with a sad countenance; but the sour faces of the multitude, like their sweet faces, have no deep cause, but are put on and off as the wind blows and a newspaper directs. Yet is the discontent of the multitude more formidable than that of the senate and the college. It is easy enough for a firm man who knows the world to brook the rage of the cultivated classes. Their rage is decorous and prudent, for they are timid as being very vulnerable themselves. But when to their feminine rage the indignation of the people is added, when the ignorant and the poor are aroused, when the unintelligent brute force that lies at the bottom of society is made to growl and mow, it needs the habit of magnanimity and religion to treat it godlike as a trifle of no concernment."

156 Maggie Miller, "Facebook to label but leave up 'newsworthy' posts that violate policies." The Hill, June 26, 2020 https://thehill.com/policy/technology/504750-facebook-to-label-newsworthy-posts-that-violate-policies

157 Tyler Sonnemaker, "Facebook removed a Trump post because it violated the company's policies banning 'harmful COVID misinformation,'" Business Insider, August 5, 2020. https://www.businessinsider.com/facebook-removed-trump-post-containing-

harmful-covid-misinformation-2020-8

158 https://www.facebook.com/zuck/posts/10112270823363411?utm_source=CJR%20Daily%20News&utm_campaign=20f92b86e9-EMAIL_CAMPAIGN_2018_10_31_05_02_COPY_01&utm_medium=email&utm_term=0_9c93f57676-20f92b86e9-174377885&mc_cid=20f92b86e9&mc_eid=97627f6796

159 J. Edward Moreno, "Google bans Zero Hedge from its advertising platform, issues citation against The Federalist," The Hill, June 16, 2020. https://thehill.com/policy/technology/503013-google-banned-the-federalist-and-zerohedge-from-its-advertising-platform

160 Todd Spangler, "Google Says It Did Not Ban Right-Wing Site The Federalist From Ad Network Over Racist Content," Variety, June 16, 2020 https://variety.com/2020/digital/news/google-federalist-ad-network-ban-1234637386/

161 https://www.youtube.com/watch?v=_RRaCmffClg

162 Zachary Evans, "Google Threatens to Ban the Federalist from Generating Ad Revenue after Intervention by NBC News, National Review, June 16, 2020 https://www.nationalreview.com/news/google-bans-the-federalist-from-generating-ad-revenue-after-intervention-by-nbc-news/?utm_source=email&utm_medium=breaking&utm_campaign=newstrack&utm_term=20638691

163 See endnote 29.

164 Ibid.

165 Rod McGuirk, "Australia to make Google and Facebook pay for news content," AP, April 20, 2020 https://apnews.com/8ca7559d39b89d097a158043ca8f44bc?utm_source=piano&utm_medium=email&utm_campaign=morningwire&pnespid=ifZ.rP9TFAKNYUWPXXzDzZD8sJLg4RKUew_Hgt1w

166 "Q&A: eBay Advertising exec on real intent, cookies and new tech," Smart Brief, May 27, 2020 https://www.smartbrief.com/original/2020/05/qa-ebay-advertising-exec-real-intent-cookies-and-new-tech?utm_source=Briefs&utm_medium=FeaturedContent&utm_campaign=Q2Blog

167 Brad Bender, A new licensing program to support the news industry, Google News Initiative, June 25, 2020 https://www.blog.google/outreach-initiatives/google-news-initiative/licensing-program-support-news-industry-/?utm_source=CJR+Daily+News&utm_campaign=3c80fac650-EMAIL_CAMPAIGN_2018_10_31_05_02_COPY_01&utm_medium=email&utm_term=0_9c93f57676-3c80fac650-174377885&mc_cid=3c80fac650&mc_eid=97627f6796

168 Building a Stronger Future for Journalism, Google News Initiative https://newsinitiative.withgoogle.com/

169 Providing emergency funding for 5,300+ local news organizations, Google News Initiative https://www.blog.google/outreach-initiatives/google-news-initiative/providing-emergency-funding-5300-local-news-orgs/

170 Jacob S. Hacker, The Great Risk Shift The New Economic Insecurity and the Decline of the American Dream https://global.oup.com/academic/product/the-great-risk-shift-9780190844141?cc=us&lang=en&

171 Hugh Carter Donahue, "Pope Francis, public policy and 21st century wealth creation," The Hill, October 1, 2015 https://thehill.com/blogs/congress-blog/economy-budget/255557-pope-francis-public-policy-and-21st-century-wealth

172 What Life Means to Einstein An Interview by George Sylvester Viereck, The Saturday Evening Post, October 26, 1929. http://www.saturdayeveningpost.com/wp-content/uploads/satevepost/what_life_means_to_einstein.pdf

173 The numbers are arresting.
In its most recent survey on wealth in the United States, the Saint Louis Federal Reserve Bank reports that 50% of Americans, approximately 63,000,000 families, hold 1% of $86.6T national wealth; that is, $867B, approximately $13,761.00/family.
As it is now, all the attention goes to peddling advertising to the top 10%; that is 12.6 million families commanding $66.7T or $529,833,333.00/family, or the next 40%; that is 50.4 million families commanding $19T or $398,452,380.00/family.

174 Thomas Piketty, Emmanuel Saez and Gabriel Zucman, "Distributional National Accounts: Methods and Estimates for the United States," The Quarterly Journal of Economics, Vol. 133 May 2018 Issue 2 http://gabriel-zucman.eu/files/PSZ2018QJE.pdf

175 Mark Twain and Charles Dudley Warner, The Gilded Age, 1873, https://www.gutenberg.org/files/3178/3178-h/3178-h.htm

176 Mary Jo Foley, "Microsoft starts rolling out Money in Excel personal finance-management feature," ZDNet, June 15, 2020 https://www.zdnet.com/article/microsoft-starts-rolling-out-money-in-excel-personal-finance-management-feature/?ftag=TRE-03-10aaa6b&bhid=28493564473397578750343099000497&mid=12-882240&cid=2131743225

177 George S. Ford, "Subsidizing Broadband: Price, Relevance, and the Digital Divide," Phoenix Center for Advanced Legal and Economic Public Policy Studies Perspective 20-05, July 7, 2020

178 Ethan Marcotte, "Responsive Web Design," May 25, 2010. https://alistapart.com/article/responsive-web-design/

179 Dr Johnny Ryan, "Understanding the Digital Advertising Ecosystem and the Impact of Data Privacy and Competition Policy," Senate Judiciary Committee https://www.judiciary.senate.gov/imo/media/doc/Ryan%20Testimony.pdf

180 O'Kelley testimony, Senate Judiciary Committee, https://www.judiciary.senate.gov/imo/media/doc/O'Kelley%20Testimony.pdf

181 A thoughtful colloquy memorializes Ryan's engagement with Brave in August, 2020.

182 https://brave.com/wp-content/uploads/2019/06/DCN-letter-re-Brave-case-FINAL.pdf

183 Gregory Barber, "Facebook's Cryptocurrency Might Work Like Loyalty Points A report says Facebook is seeking investors for its planned cryptocurrency, and merchants who might accept the virtual coin," Wired, May 3, 2019. https://www.wired.com/story/facebooks-cryptocurrency-might-work-like-loyalty-points/

184 Zachary Warmbrodt, "Maxine Waters threatens Facebook's cryptocurrency plans, Politico, July 8, 2019 https://www.politico.com/story/2019/07/08/facebook-cryptocurrency-maxine-waters-1571234

185 See endnote 180.

186 David Siegel and Rob Reich, "It's Not Too Late for Social Media to Regulate Itself Opinion: A self-regulatory organization for search and social media—like the financial industry's FINRA—would protect the public interest without enacting overly blunt laws that discourage innovation," Wired, February 7, 2019. https://www.wired.com/story/its-not-too-late-for-social-media-to-regulate-itself/

187 Bank of International Settlements, Annual Report, 2019 https://www.bis.org/publ/arpdf/ar2019e.pdf

188 Ester Kim, "Shut Down Cryptocurrencies' says Joseph Stiglitz as Fiat Markets Tumble," bitcoinist.com, May 6, 2019 https://bitcoinist.com/joseph-stiglitz-bitcoin-shut-down-cryptocurrencies/

189 Securities and Exchange Commission v. 1Pool Ltd. a.k.a. 1 Brocker and Patrick Brunner, U.S. District Court for the District of Columbia, https://cdn.crowdfundinsider.com/wp-content/uploads/2018/09/SEC-v.-1Pool-and-Patrick-Brunner.pdf

190 Commodity Futures Trading Commission v. 1Pool Ltd. and Patrick Brunner Trust Company Complex "United States District Court for the District of Columbia, https://cdn.crowdfundinsider.com/wp-content/uploads/2018/09/CFTC-v.-1Pool-and-Patrick-Brunner.pdf

191 Rebecca Ungarino, "Introducing 'JPM Coin': JPMorgan will be the first major US bank to launch its own cryptocurrency," Business Insider, February 14, 2019, https://markets.businessinsider.com/currencies/news/jpmorgan-cryptocurrency-launch-jpm-coin-a-first-for-a-major-us-bank-2019-2-1027953761

192 Richard Kastelein, "220 Partners at JPMorgan's Blockchain Project," Bitcoin News, April 23, 2019, https://www.the-blockchain.com/2019/04/23/220-partners-at-jpmorgans-blockchain-project-new-features/

193 Catalin Cimpanu, "$145 million funds frozen after death of cryptocurrency exchange admin Highly unlikely that the exchange and its users will ever get access to these funds ever again," Blockchain, February 3, 2019 https://www.zdnet.com/article/145-million-funds-frozen-after-death-of-cryptocurrency-exchange-admin/

194 Alexandra Frean, "Bitcoin Will Become the World's Chief Currency," The Times, March 21, 2018 https://www.thetimes.co.uk/article/bitcoin-will-become-the-worlds-single-currency-tech-chief-says-66slm0p6b

195 In the Matter of the Inquiry by Letitia James, Attorney General of the State of New York, Petitioner, Pursuant to article 23-A of the New York General Business Law in regard to the acts and practices of iFINEX INC., BFXNA INC., BFXWW INC., TETHER HOLDINGS LIMITED, TETHER OPERATIONS LIMITED, TETHER LIMITED, TETHER INTERNATIONAL LIMITED, Supreme Court of the State of New York County of New York, April 24, 2019, https://ag.ny.gov/sites/default/files/2019.04.24_signed_order.pdf

196 White Paper v2.0 | From the Libra Association Members, https://libra.org/en-US/white-paper/

197 John McAfee The GHOST Distributed exchange is now live: https://ghostx.live 1:33 PM · Jun 21, 2020 Twitter for Android

198 https://ghostx.live/#/createWallet

199 https://ripple.com/company/

200 The Internet of Value: What It Means and How It Benefits Everyone, June 21, 2017, https://ripple.com/insights/the-internet-of-value-what-it-means-and-how-it-benefits-everyone/

201 The Big Idea Hip-hop, bitcoin and stimulus checks: How Square's Cash App became a $40B business, The Hustle, September 7, 2020. news.thehustle.com

202 Examining Regulatory Frameworks for Digital Currencies and Blockchain, U.S. Senate Committee on Banking, Housing, and Urban Affairs, https://www.banking.senate.gov/hearings/examining-regulatory-frameworks-for-digital-currencies-and-blockchain

203 Linda Lacina, Thoughtful blockchain implementation is key to improving supply chains in a post-COVID world, World Economic Forum, April 28, 2020 https://www.weforum.org/agenda/2020/04/blockchain-development-toolkit-implementation-supply-chains-in-a-post-covid-world/

204 Fabio Panetta, Beyond monetary policy – protecting the continuity and safety of payments during the coronavirus crisis, European Central Bank, April 28, 2020 https://www.ecb.europa.eu/press/blog/date/2020/html/ecb.blog200428~328d7ca065. en.html?utm_source=ecb_twitter&utm_medium=social&utm_campaign=200428_FP_ blog&utm_term=blog

205 Rochelle Antoniewicz & Jane Heinrichs, "Understanding Exchange-Traded Funds: How ETFs Work," ICI Research Perspective 20, No. 5 (Sept. 2014) "On most trading days, the vast majority of ETFs do not have any primary market activity—that is, they do not create or redeem shares" cited in SEC ETF ruling.

206 Securities and Exchange Commission, Exchange Traded Funds Final Rule https://www.sec.gov/rules/final/2019/33-10695.pdf

207 Ibid.

208 Will Douglas Heaven, "This know-it-all AI learns by reading the entire web nonstop," Technology Review, September 4, 2020. https://www.technologyreview. com/2020/09/04/1008156/knowledge-graph-ai-reads-web-machine-learning-natural-language-processing/?truid=34c11974240e0124ba6c93ae303185cc&utm_ source=the_download&utm_medium=email&utm_campaign=the_download.unpaid. engagement&utm_term=non-subs&utm_content=09-07-2020

209 Ralph Waldo Emerson, "Man The Reformer," A Lecture read before the Mechanics' Apprentices' Library Association, Boston, January 25, 1841 https:// emersoncentral.com/texts/nature-addresses-lectures/lectures/man-the-reformer/

210 Charles River Bridge v. Warren Bridge, 36 U.S. 420 (1837) https://supreme.justia. com/cases/federal/us/36/420/ The litigation addresses whether a state government can grant a fresh charter to a new entrant investing and constructing infrastructure, specially a bridge across the Charles River from Boston to Charlestown, authorizing competition in bridge tolls damaging the monopoly position, granted by the state many years earlier, of the incumbent bridge owner. Chief Justice Taney and the majority rule that competition in the public interest matters more than the incumbent bridge monopolist's long standing contract. In a withering dissent, Justice Joseph Story upholds contracts.

"Whenever the grant is upon a valuable consideration, the rule of construction ceases; and the grant is expounded exactly as it would be in the case of a private grant—favorably to the grantee. Why is this rule adopted? Plainly, because the grant is a contract, and is to be interpreted according to its fair meaning. It would be to the dishonor of the government, that it should pocket a fair consideration, and then quibble as to the obscurities and implications of its own contract. Such was the doctrine of my Lord COKE, and of the venerable sages of the law, in other times, when a resistance to prerogative was equivalent to a removal from office. Even in the worst ages of arbitrary power, and irresistible prerogative, they did not hesitate to declare, that contracts founded in a valuable consideration ought to be construed liberally for the subject, for the honor of the crown. 2 Inst. 496. See also Com. Dig.

Franchise, C. F. 6. If we are to have the grants of the legislature construed by the rules applicable to royal grants, it is but common justice, to follow them throughout, for the honor of this republic. The justice of the commonwealth will not, I trust, be deemed less extensive than that of the crown.... If, then, the present were the case of a royal grant, I should most strenuously contend, both upon principle and authority, that it was to receive a liberal, and not a strict construction. I should so contend, upon the plain intent of the charter, from its nature and objects, and from its burdens and duties. It is, confessedly, a case of contract, and not of bounty; a case of contract for a valuable consideration; for objects of public utility; to encourage enterprise; to advance the public convenience; and to secure a just remuneration for large outlays of private capital.... As to the manner of construing parliamentary grants for private enterprise, there are some recent decisions, which, in my judgment, establish two very important principles, applicable directly to the present case; which, if not confirmatory of the views which I have endeavored to maintain, are at least not repugnant to them. The first is, that all grants for purposes of this sort are to be construed as contracts between the government and the grantees, and not as mere laws; the second is, that they are to receive a reasonable construction; and that if, either upon their express terms, or by just inference from the terms, the intent of the contract can be made out, it is to be recognised and enforced accordingly. But if the language be ambiguous, or if the inference be not clearly made out, then the contract is to be taken most strongly against the grantor, and most favorably for the public. ... Lord TENTERDEN, in delivering the opinion of the court, said, 'this like many other cases, is a bargain between a company of adventurers and the public, the terms of which are expressed in the statute. And the rule of construction in all such cases in now fully established to be this that any ambiguity in the terms of the contract must operate against the adventurers, and in favor of the public; and the plaintiffs can claim nothing which is not clearly given to them by the act.' 'Now, it is quite certain, that the company have no right expressly given to receive any compensation, except, &c.; and therefore, it is incumbent upon them to show, that that they have a right, clearly given by inference from some other of the clauses.' This latter statement shows, that it is not indispensable, that in grants of this sort, the contract or the terms of the bargain should be in express language; it is sufficient, if they may be clearly proved by implication or inference.... We are construing a grant of the legislature, which though in the form of a statute, is still but a solemn contract.... All the learned judges in the state court admitted, that the franchise of Charles River bridge, whatever it be, could not be resumed or interfered with. The legislature could not recall its grant, or destroy it. It is a contract, whose obligation cannot be constitutionally impaired.... I go further, and maintain, not only that it is not a case for strict construction; but that the charter, upon its very face, by its terms, and for its professed objects, demands from the court, upon undeniable principles of law, a favorable construction for the grantees. In the first place, the legislature has declared, that the erecting of the bridge will be of great public utility; and this exposition of its own motives for the grant, requires the court to give a liberal interpretation, in order to promote, and not to destroy, an enterprise of great public utility. In the next place, the grant is a contract for a valuable consideration, and a full and adequate consideration. The proprietors are to lay out a large sum of money (and in those times it was a very large outlay of capital) in erecting a bridge; they are to keep it in repair, during the whole period of forty years; they are to surrender it in good repair, at the end of that period, to the state, as its own property; they are to pay, during the whole period, an annuity of 200l. to Harvard College; and they are to incur other heavy expenses and burdens, for the public accommodation. In return for all these charges, they are entitled to no more than the receipt of the tolls, during the forty years, for their reimbursement of capital, interest and expenses. With all this, they are to take upon themselves the chances of success; and if the enterprise fails, the loss is exclusively their own. Nor let any man imagine, that there was not, at the time when this charter was granted, much solid ground for doubting success. In order to entertain a just view of this subject, we must go back to that period of general bankruptcy, and distress and difficulty. The constitution of the United States was not only not then in existence, but it was not then even dreamed of. The union of the states was crumbling into ruins, under the old confederation. Agriculture, manufactures and commerce were at their lowest ebb. There was infinite danger to all the states, from local interests and jealousies, and from the apparent impossibility of a much longer adherence to that shadow of a government, the continental congress. And even four years afterwards, when every evil had been greatly aggravated, and civil war was added to other calamities, the constitution of the United States was all but shipwrecked, in passing through the state conventions; it was adopted by very slender majorities. These are historical facts, which required no coloring to give them effect, and admitted of no concealment, to seduce men into schemes of future aggrandizement. I would even now put it to the common sense of every man, whether, if the constitution of the United States had not been adopted, the charter would have been worth a forty years' purchase of the tolls. This is not all. It is well known, historically, that this was the very first bridge ever constructed, in New England, over navigable tide-waters so near the sea. The rigors of our climate, the dangers from sudden thaws and freezing, and the obstructions from ice in a rapid current, were deemed by many persons to be insuperable obstacles to the success of such a project. It was believed, that the bridge would scarcely stand a single severe winter. And I myself am old enough to know, that in regard to other arms of the sea, at much later periods, the same doubts have had a strong and depressing influence upon public enterprises. If Charles River bridge had been carried away, during the first or second season after its erection, it is far from being certain, that up to this moment, another bridge, upon such an arm of the sea, would ever have been erected in Massachusetts. I state these things, which are of public notoriety, to repel the notion that the legislature was surprised into an incautions grant, or that the reward was more than adequate to the perils. There was a full and adequate consideration, in a pecuniary sense, for the charter. But, in a more general sense, the erection of the bridge, as a matter of accommodation, has been incalcuably beneficial to the public. Unless, therefore, we are wholly to disregard the declarations of the legislature, and the objects of the charter, and the historical facts of the times; and indulge in mere private speculations of profit and loss, by our present lights and experience; it seems to me, that the court is bound to come to the interpretation of this charter, with a persuasion that it was granted in furtherance, and not in derogation, of the public good. But I do not insist upon any extraordinary liberality in interpreting this charter. All I contend for is, that it shall receive a fair and reasonable interpretation; so as to carry into effect the legislative intention, and secure to the grantees a just security for their privileges. I might, indeed, well have spared myself any investigation of the principles upon which royal and legislative grants are ordinarily to be construed; for this court has itself furnished an unequivocal rule for interpreting all public contracts.

The present grant is confessedly a contract; and in Huidekoper's Lessee v. Douglass, 3 Cranch 1, this court said: 'This is a contract, and although a state is a party, it ought to be construed according to those well-established principles which regulate contracts, generally;' that is, precisely as in cases between mere private persons, taking into consideration the nature and objects of the grant. A like rule was adopted by this court, in the case of a contract by the United States. United States v. Gurney, 4 Cranch 333. And the good sense and justice of the rule seem equally irresistible."
https://www.law.cornell.edu/supremecourt/text/36/420

211 Ibid.
212 Ralph Waldo Emerson, "Wealth," The Conduct of Life (1860), https://emersoncentral.com/texts/the-conduct-of-life/wealth/ 1860

213 William Penn, SOME ACCOUNT OF THE PROVINCE Of PENNSYLVANIA IN AMERICA; Lately Granted under the Great Seal Of ENGLAND To William Penn, &c. Together with the Privileges and Powers necessary to the well-governing thereof. Made Public for the Information of such as are or may be disposed to Transport themselves or Servants into those Parts. LONDON: Printed, and Sold by Benjamin Clark, Bookseller in George Yard, Lombard Street, 1681.